FiGHT to WIN!

Also by Kim Kelly

Fight Like Hell: The Untold History of American Labor

FIGHT to WIN!

Heroes of American Labor

The Young Readers Edition of FIGHT LIKE HELL

Kim Kelly

Simon & Schuster Books for Young Readers
NEW YORK AMSTERDAM/ANTWERP LONDON
TORONTO SYDNEY/MELBOURNE NEW DELHI

SIMON & SCHUSTER BOOKS FOR YOUNG READERS
An imprint of Simon & Schuster Children's Publishing Division
1230 Avenue of the Americas, New York, New York 10020
For more than 100 years, Simon & Schuster has championed authors and the stories they create. By respecting the copyright of an author's intellectual property, you enable Simon & Schuster and the author to continue publishing exceptional books for years to come. We thank you for supporting the author's copyright by purchasing an authorized edition of this book.
No amount of this book may be reproduced or stored in any format, nor may it be uploaded to any website, database, language-learning model, or other repository, retrieval, or artificial intelligence system without express permission. All rights reserved. Inquiries may be directed to Simon & Schuster, 1230 Avenue of the Americas, New York, NY 10020
or permissions@simonandschuster.com.
Text © 2022, 2025 by Kim Kelly
Jacket illustration © 2025 by Vesna Asanovic
This young readers edition is adapted from *Fight Like Hell* by Kim Kelly, published by One Signal Publishers in 2022.
All rights reserved, including the right of reproduction in whole or in part in any form.
SIMON & SCHUSTER BOOKS FOR YOUNG READERS
and related marks are trademarks of Simon & Schuster, LLC.
For information about special discounts for bulk purchases, please contact Simon & Schuster Special Sales at 1-866-506-1949 or business@simonandschuster.com.
Simon & Schuster strongly believes in freedom of expression and stands against censorship in all its forms. For more information, visit BooksBelong.com.
The Simon & Schuster Speakers Bureau can bring authors to your live event. For more information or to book an event, contact the Simon & Schuster Speakers Bureau at 1-866-248-3049 or visit our website at www.simonspeakers.com.
Interior design by Hilary Zarycky
The text for this book was set in Adobe Caslon Pro.
Manufactured in the United States of America
0325 BVG
First Edition
2 4 6 8 10 9 7 5 3 1
Library of Congress Cataloging-in-Publication Data
Names: Kelly, Kim (Journalist), author. Title: Fight to win! : heroes of American labor / Kim Kelly. Description: [New York] : [Simon and Schuster Books for Young Readers], [2025] | Includes bibliographical references and index. | Audience term: Children | Audience: Ages 10+ | Summary: "Freed Black women organizing for protection in the Reconstruction-era South. Jewish immigrant garment workers braving deadly conditions for a sliver of independence. Asian American fieldworkers rejecting government-sanctioned indentured servitude across the Pacific. Incarcerated workers advocating for basic human rights and fair wages. The queer Black labor leader who helped orchestrate America's civil rights movement. These are only some of the working-class heroes who propelled American labor's relentless push for fairness and equal protection under the law. In this well-researched work of journalism, *Teen Vogue* columnist and independent labor reporter Kim Kelly excavates our history and shows how the rights the American worker has today—the forty-hour workweek, workplace-safety standards, restrictions on child labor, protection from harassment and discrimination on the job—were earned with literal blood, sweat, and tears.
Inspirational, intersectional, and full of crucial lessons from the past, *Fight to Win!* shows what is possible when the working class demands the dignity it has always deserved"—Provided by publisher.
Identifiers: LCCN 2024041700 | ISBN 9781665937290 (hardcover) | ISBN 9781665937306 (paperback) | ISBN 9781665937313 (ebook) | Subjects: LCSH: Employee rights—United States—Juvenile literature. | Activism—United States—Juvenile literature. Classification: LCC HD6971.8 .K45 2025 | DDC 331.8092/520973—dc23/eng/20250208
LC record available at https://lccn.loc.gov/2024041700

For Sai, Averi, Jack, Max, and all the other young troublemakers out there fighting to build a better world.

TABLE OF CONTENTS

INTRODUCTION	1
SARAH BAGLEY	17
BEN FLETCHER	29
CLARA LEMLICH	41
FRANCES PERKINS	57
LUCY PARSONS	73
MOTHER JONES	87
EUGENE V. DEBS	102
ROSINA TUCKER	120
MARIA MORENO	133
AH QUON MCELRATH	145
SUE KO LEE	156
MAIDA SPRINGER KEMP	168
EMMA TENAYUCA	179
DOROTHY BOLDEN	192
BAYARD RUSTIN	203
NAGI DAIFULLAH	217

Judy Heumann	**224**
Silme Domingo and Gene Viernes	**239**
Joni Christian	**250**
Bhairavi Desai	**256**
Jennifer Bates	**265**
Labor's Next Chapter	**278**
Acknowledgments	**285**
Chapter Sources	**287**
Photos	**307**
About the Author	**311**

INTRODUCTION

The first time I met Jennifer Bates, she was almost as nervous as I was. One of us had racked up a decent amount of on-camera experience by then, but you wouldn't have guessed who it was by looking at us. She was dressed in a royal-blue blouse and black overcoat, her hair and makeup impeccable. Meanwhile, I trailed behind her in my grubby Carhartt jacket and braids. It was a moody gray day in early February 2021, and I'd just arrived in Alabama for my first big reporting trip since the COVID-19 pandemic hit. I hadn't left my home in Philadelphia for more than a year and I was still a little nervous about getting up close and personal with anyone. With that in mind, I figured that holding interviews outside on a park bench was the best-case scenario. A digital media nonprofit called More Perfect Union had sent me there to cover a story that was developing in an Amazon warehouse a few miles down the road, in a struggling town called Bessemer.

Once known as the "Marvel City," Bessemer had fallen down on its luck. The city was once a major manufacturing region, but over the years, business had dried up. Alabama's $7.25 minimum wage made it difficult for workers to turn their noses up at any kind of work that paid a little better, so Amazon's promise of $15 an hour appeared to be a step up. It wasn't until the warehouse opened in March 2020—just as the pandemic had begun—that the people hired to spend their days inside the concrete fortress on a hill began to realize what exactly it was that they had signed up for. They quickly realized they needed to do something about it, together. By the summer, the workers there had decided to unionize.

If the workers won, their union would be a first for Amazon's massive U.S. operations. Folks in the labor movement also hoped a win in Bessemer would inspire the hundreds of thousands of workers in the company's 110 other U.S. warehouse facilities to get organized, too. Past efforts to unionize at Amazon had had mixed results, though. It turns out going up against one of the richest men in the world was pretty tough, especially when he really, really didn't want you to win! Amazon CEO Jeff Bezos and his executives cracked down on organizing wherever possible, but workers had made small gains here and there.

In 2018, Somali American and Somali immigrant workers in Minnesota successfully forced Amazon warehouses to improve their working conditions and respect their religious needs. Amazon workers in more union-friendly countries like Germany, Italy, Poland, France, and Spain had been able to unionize, too, but Alabama was another story. Its state and local politicians were all very blunt about their anti-union position, and it was always going to be an uphill battle to unionize the warehouse there. It was going to take something big and bold and visionary to finally crack Amazon's armor. In 2020, that moment arrived—and it was being led by a group of middle-aged Black warehouse workers in a struggling Alabama town whose union roots ran as deep as the coal mines just a few miles down the road.

Other journalists have been covering Amazon, its labor offenses, and its rotten business ethics for years, but this would be my chance to be the first reporter on the ground for what may be an important new chapter in the story. I had been hired to narrate and produce video coverage, which, as a lifelong writer, I saw as a fun new challenge. This particular story was fascinating on many levels and so potentially significant for labor's future that I couldn't turn it down, even if I was anxious. No one had predicted then how huge the campaign would become, or how much of my own life would come to revolve around its ups and downs. My biggest priority that day was to find out what Jennifer Bates and her coworkers wanted the rest of us to know about their fight.

We said our hellos in the union hall's parking lot before piling back into our respective cars and heading over to Birmingham's Civil Rights District to choose an interview location. Jennifer was a striking, soft-spoken woman; she was shy, but she was determined, and I could see it in her eyes the moment we met. I also could sense that she was deeply kind, but not inclined to suffer fools. We walked through a park across from the famous Sixteenth Street Baptist Church, where four little Black girls had been murdered by the Ku Klux Klan just a few years before Jennifer was born. Her black coat billowed in the wind beneath the watchful eye of a statue of Dr. Martin Luther King Jr. History was alive in that park, and in that city, and in the campaign that Bates and her coworkers had launched. The civil rights leader's final action before his life was extinguished by a sniper's bullet had been in service to labor. He'd spent his last day speaking to a crowd of striking unionized sanitation workers in Memphis, Tennessee, who were demanding respect for themselves and their coworkers.

Bates emphasized that connection once the camera started rolling. Dr. King was a union man, and the Amazon workers of Bessemer saw themselves as following in his footsteps on the long road toward justice. Like him, Bates was guided by her faith. "If it is meant to be, God is gonna make sure it comes to pass—and if it doesn't, then there was something in there that we should have learned," she told me later on. "We are supposed to learn out of it."

I knew I was asking a lot from her that day. She was about to go on record about what had driven her and her coworkers to go up against one of the most powerful companies in the world. Amazon: whose economic power was inconceivable, their reputation for cruelty and retaliation was legendary, and their political influence was everywhere. I was just there to bear witness. Her story would soon become national news, her face would soon grace the pages of major publications, and her struggle would inspire millions—but right then, it was just her and me, sitting on a park bench, talking about the pain in her legs and the fire in her heart. As the old saying goes, the cause of labor is the hope of the world, and as we spoke, that hope shined hard in Bates's deep brown eyes. I could feel the heat roll off her words.

No great labor leader works alone, and Bates was no exception. Her coworker Daryl Richardson was there too that day, telling me about the grueling conditions and overwhelming feeling of unfairness that had led him to take action. Like Bates, he had had prior experience with unions, and had seen firsthand the impact they could have on righting wrongs and pushing for change in a flawed workplace. After some quick Googling, Richardson placed the fateful call that ended up drawing a small army of Retail, Wholesale and Department Store Union (RWDSU) organizers down to Bessemer. That phone call launched one of the most-watched, hardest-fought union election campaigns in recent U.S. history. A gentle man with a warm heart, he had made the 40-minute drive from his home in Tuscaloosa to the Amazon warehouse in Bessemer and then to the RWDSU union hall in downtown Birmingham more times than he could remember.

The footage from those interviews ended up in a series of videos that racked up millions of views, and drew lots of attention from folks who were horrified to see what was really going on inside those warehouses. More importantly, union organizers in Bessemer sent them around to the workers themselves to help counteract Amazon's anti-union messaging. They faced an uphill battle there. By the time I arrived, Amazon had already spent months plastering anti-union banners throughout the warehouse, sending anti-union messages to workers' personal phones, and even hanging flyers in the same bathroom stalls that workers barely had time to visit during their backbreaking ten-hour shifts. Worse, Amazon had taken to forcing workers to attend captive-audience meetings, in which high-priced "union avoidance" consultants tried to persuade the workers they were better off without a union and lectured them about the evils of organized labor. Those who spoke up in favor of the union were kicked out, or targeted with one-on-one lectures on the shop floor. As unfair as it was, captive-audience meetings were legal under the United

States's outdated labor laws. Anti-union bosses love them, because it gives them an opportunity to scare workers and feed them misinformation. But as the media attention increased, more workers became comfortable with the idea of speaking out publicly. Momentum began to build. What started as a trickle turned into a flood.

As the Bessemer union drive picked up steam, journalists from around the country and across the globe parachuted into Birmingham to follow the story. I kept coming back, making three trips in as many months; as soon as I'd get home, I'd start planning ways to get back to Alabama as soon as I could. More workers took the microphone, like Emmit Ashford and Linda Burns. Organizers like Michael "Big Mike" Foster, a RWDSU member and poultry plant worker, became a beloved figure, and was eventually hired by the union.

The Amazon union drive became front-page news. When the campaign finally came to an end and the votes began to be counted, the *New York Times* even ran a vote tracker with live updates. Momentum had picked up even more before the election. The weekend before, Senator Bernie Sanders and rapper-activist Killer Mike had traveled to Alabama to whip up enthusiasm for the union. As the deadline neared, all eyes were on Bessemer.

Despite the massive roadblocks in their way, after seeing everything that Jennifer and Daryl and everyone else had poured into this election, after witnessing firsthand the excitement and energy around it, after meeting the dozens of locals and out-of-towners alike who had dedicated months of their time to boosting the union drive, after reading the coverage around it and doing my own reporting for months, I never even imagined that they wouldn't win.

But then . . . they didn't. When the final tally came out, Amazon had won after all, beating out the union by a wide margin. Jennifer Bates and the other pro-union workers at that Bessemer warehouse had fallen short this time, but the fight did not stop there. RWDSU immediately filed almost two dozen objections against Amazon with the National Labor Relations Board, calling out the company's unfair labor practices. In 2022, a second election was run. For a second time, the effort failed, and the union again filed a raft of charges against Amazon. As I write this, the results of that second election remain tied up in court, and workers at that Bessemer warehouse have continued their organizing efforts. Five years since Daryl made that phone call, they still haven't given up on winning their union.

When I spoke to Bates the day after the first election vote tally came out, she made it clear that she and her coworkers weren't ready to back down. She didn't try to hide her disappointment or her suspicions that Amazon had used dirty tactics to undermine the election. But what was most clear was her enduring hope. Her eyes were still full of the same determination and faith that I'd seen when we first met.

She wasn't nervous to talk to me this time, either. Since those first few interviews in February 2021, she has given hundreds more, appeared in front of dozens of cameras, spoken at countless meetings with her coworkers, met with celebrities and politicians, and testified in front of Congress. The David-and-Goliath fight that consumed her life for months never consumed her spirit. That, she gave freely and abundantly to the cause, like so many other labor leaders before her. Jennifer Bates was a woman with nothing left to fear but her creator, and as far as she was concerned, Jeff Bezos was a mere speck of dust beneath her sandals.

A lot has changed since that first Amazon vote in Alabama. They may still be waiting for their win, but the impact of what those workers accomplished reverberated throughout the labor movement, and set an important precedent. As I wrote back in 2021, "Someone had to be the first, and now the next group of workers who decide to take a moonshot of their own and go toe-to-toe with a giant will get even closer." A few months after I turned in the manuscript for the first version of the adult edition, titled *Fight Like Hell*, that prediction came true. Workers at an Amazon warehouse in Staten Island, led by former and current Amazon workers Christian Smalls, Derrick Palmer, Angelika Maldonado, Michelle Valentin

Nieves, and all the others on their committee of worker-organizers, successfully unionized as the independent Amazon Labor Union. It was an explosive victory and has given so many other workers in this country hope. What the ALU accomplished (and are continuing to fight for) shows the constant work of progress and revolution, of pushing forward, further, and further still. It's the unfinished business of centuries of fighters and thinkers and dreamers. Each generation brings us just a little bit closer to the dream, until we can finally see liberation up ahead.

I've been lucky. I grew up in a working-class, blue-collar, rural union household. My dad, grandpa, and uncles all worked construction. My granddad was a millwright in a steel mill, and my grandma was a teacher. The union was a constant presence in my home, as much a part of our lives as my dad's gray pickup truck or the pine trees out back. I remember the times when my dad was on strike, and how we had to tighten our belts until the conflict ended and he was back on his regular pay. When I was 17 and my mom got really sick, her surgery bills topped the quarter-million mark; the health insurance his union provided kept us from going bankrupt.

Of course I also remember him complaining about long, boring union meetings, which is funny to think about now that I've been to literally hundreds of them myself. My dad's never been good at sitting still, so I don't blame him for that. Sure, he might not have liked the less exciting parts of union membership, but he instilled in me the unshakable idea that the union was a good thing to have—and that when your boss was doing you wrong, you could count on the union to have your back. Every worker deserves to feel that way. Thanks to forces beyond their control, though, so many continue to be denied that protection at Amazon and in countless other workplaces across the U.S.

In the following pages, I'm going to introduce you to many more versions of Jennifer Bates, individuals who have made waves across class and gender and race and time. Some of them were famous during their own eras, and then forgotten; others were never given the spotlight they deserved at all because of who they were, where they were born, or who they loved. All of them have made incredibly important contributions to the history of the U.S. and especially to the history of working people. My hope is that you will see yourself or someone you love in their stories, and that learning about them will give you the courage you need to stick up for yourself or your coworkers someday. I'm so excited for you to meet them!

Fight to Win! is not going to be a comprehensive, nuts-and-bolts account of the entire U.S. labor movement from start to end. That would require about a thousand more pages, at least! You'll probably notice some pretty big omissions, and while I would have liked to include people from every single industry and profession, I had to pick a few favorites to make sure this book ever got finished. I'm not an academic or trained historian, either, so I'm very grateful to those who are. This book would not exist without the hard work of the academics, historians, researchers, and archivists who first chronicled this history and wrote important books about it that ensured that these stories were preserved.

Every story is a labor story, and every labor story builds on years—if not centuries—of previous organizing victories and failures. With this book, I wanted to make space for stories that don't always get covered, and for people whose incredible contributions to the cause have largely been forgotten by history. The stories of poor and working-class women, Black people, Latino people, Indigenous people, Asian and Pacific Islander people, immigrants of all backgrounds, religious minorities, queer and trans people, disabled people, and people who are incarcerated don't always get the attention they deserve when they're still with us. It's a shame, too, because those are the very people who had the most to lose but found it within themselves to give more and fight harder than anyone else.

Working people have always been essential, but this country has often failed to recognize the value of their lives as well as their labor. Starting in 2020, when the COVID-19 pandemic pushed workers onto the front lines and pushed our society to its breaking point, labor actions swept the nation. Millions were either left jobless or forced to risk catching a deadly disease without adequate protection. Workers whose labor keeps society running—the janitors and cleaning staff, the farmworkers and meatpackers, the grocery store workers and public transit operators, the delivery drivers and postal service workers—were given no choice but to work through it. They deserved every bit of praise they received, but it shouldn't have taken a global health crisis for the government to start taking their needs seriously.

So many of the people whose jobs were newly recognized as "essential" toiled in industries that lacked labor protections. "Those people, not only do they not have a safety net, but no matter what is going on, they have to continue to put their bodies and lives on the line," Veena Dubal, a law professor at the University of California, Irvine, and a fierce advocate for workers told me. "There's some great tragic irony that it's these 'essential workers' who are the most dispossessed: the people who are carved out of all [labor] protections, the people who do the most dangerous work, and the people whose lifespans are the shortest as a result."

They were not, and still have not been, paid a livable wage, still cannot afford healthcare, and are still disenfranchised by a deeply flawed system that places people of color and undocumented workers at increased risk, whether there's a pandemic raging or not. People incarcerated in jails and prisons were forced to manufacture masks, gowns, and hand sanitizer for use outside the walls, even as the virus turned those very facilities into death traps. Prisoners were called on to dig graves for those who were lost to the virus, and watched their own friends get sicker.

Those in the medical field—doctors, nurses, hospital technicians, hospital janitors and laundry workers, funeral home owners and morticians—were endangered by personal protective equipment shortages. The entire awful situation exposed the hazardous conditions that have been allowed to fester under the U.S.'s cruel capitalist system. By hitting the streets and raising the alarm, workers started fighting back.

Now it seems like more workers than ever are imagining a better way, and looking to the past for inspiration. Pro-union sentiment rose to 71 percent in 2022, the highest that mark has been since 1965. The United States's labor laws are outdated, the National Labor Relations Board is understaffed and underfunded, but there is a great and mighty wave of organizing happening regardless. From fast food to academia to museums to mines to digital media to tech, workers in industry after industry are taking control, forcing bosses to the table, and fighting for their piece of the pie. There is a vital sense of urgency that has only increased with every new crisis. Something's got to give.

One of my favorite historical labor figures, Elizabeth Gurley Flynn, hit the nail on the head way back in the early 20th century. She was talking about the need to keep political and social justice demands on the same level as so-called bread-and-butter economic issues. In her words: "What is a labor victory? I maintain that it is a twofold thing. Workers must gain economic advantage, but they must also gain revolutionary spirit, in order to achieve a complete victory. For workers to gain a few cents more a day, a few minutes less a day, and go back to work with the same psychology, the same attitude toward society, is to achieve a temporary gain and not a lasting victory." In other words, a raise in wages isn't enough. Workers need—and deserve—so much more.

Every worker today stands on the shoulders of giants. You will meet some of them here, like Lucy Parsons, Maria Moreno, Bayard Rustin, and Eugene V. Debs. Most people won't even recognize their names, though, which is exactly why we need to get their history into people's hands now—and that starts with you, the person reading this book! These folks understood that they might not win everything they wanted, but they could at least try to push things a little bit further ahead. Bit by bit, day by day, year by year, they and their descendants have seen some of those dreams come true, from the eight-hour workday to a federal minimum wage to laws against child labor. If they hadn't dreamed as big and fought as hard as they did, our world would look a lot different—and honestly, it would be a whole lot worse. Thanks to those who came before us, we now have the opportunity to build upon their work and leave the world in better shape than we found it.

Some of the stories in this book will break your heart. Some will make you angry. Some will make you laugh, or shake your head, or raise your fist in triumph. The people within these pages were tough, determined, messy, and complicated human beings just like you and me. They weren't perfect, they made mistakes, they lost campaigns and caused trouble. They also cared deeply about their fellow workers, and refused to back down when it felt like the entire world was against them. I hope you find inspiration in their stories and take the lessons they taught us to heart. When the day comes that *you're* at work, and *your* boss treats you or one of your coworkers unfairly, remember their names. They fought to win—and so can you.

It's on each and every one of us to carry the torch forward. As the song "Solidarity Forever" says, we can bring to birth a new world from the ashes of the old. And as Jennifer Bates would tell you herself, "Burn, let it burn."

Sarah Bagley
The Determined Mill Girl
1837–1846

Let us trust on and try to leave a little seed on earth that shall bear fruit when we shall pass away.

When Sarah Bagley walked through the doors of the Hamilton Manufacturing Company on her first day in 1837, she could scarcely believe her ears. It was so loud! Everywhere around her, noisy pieces of machinery called power looms whirred and spit out strands of cotton thread. Young women just like her operated the spinning machines and scurried around with bundles of cloth. The thunderous racket filled the room, and seemed to never stop. It couldn't have been more different from the quiet fields and green forests of her hometown in Candia, New Hampshire. But that was exactly why Sarah was there. Like so many other young women of her era, she wanted more than a quiet domestic life. She was looking for an adventure—or at least, a taste of freedom.

At first, Sarah loved her new job. She had been excited to leave her sleepy hometown and move to bustling

Lowell, Massachusetts, to work as a weaver in one of the city's textile mills (big factories where fabric like cotton was manufactured). It wasn't just about her own desires, either; her family had fallen on hard times, and she needed the money to help them out. The Industrial Revolution was in full swing, and Sarah was right there in the middle of it. It was a time of huge social and economic change. For example, in 1837, when Sarah moved to Lowell, it was still unusual for a woman like her—a white, New England farm girl from a rural family—to have a job at all. Most women in her position were expected to stay home, get married, and care for their children. Her life had already been planned out for her since the moment she was born. But the world had opened up since then, and Sarah became part of a new generation of young women who were leaving home and traveling to industrial cities across New England to find work in factories.

Factory owners liked hiring young women to work in their mills; they thought that the "mill girls" would only stay for a few years before leaving to get married. Factory owners also assumed that young women were weak, obedient, and willing to accept much lower wages than their male counterparts. Like many of her coworkers, Sarah didn't have time to think about gender equality; she was just excited to jump into her new life and start earning her 50-cent daily wage. When she got to Lowell, she rented a room in a company-owned boardinghouse alongside several other young women workers. Sarah was a little older than most of her new friends; she was 31 when she started, but still had to obey the "house matron" who monitored the young women's behavior.

Working in the mills gave many a new sense of independence. It wasn't true freedom, but for that first wave of women, who would have otherwise been doomed to lives of isolation or domestic drudgery, it was at least something *new*. For the first time in their lives, women like Sarah were able to earn their own money and decide how to spend their free time. What little time they had away from the factory was entirely their own, with no parents, siblings, or farm animals demanding their attention. Their paychecks also gave them room to dream: to save up for college or future weddings, to buy nice clothes and accessories, and to help support their families. The mill girls also enjoyed cultural activities, and were far more intellectual than the mill bosses assumed. They attended lectures from thinkers like Ralph Waldo Emerson and Henry David Thoreau, formed debate teams and political clubs, and started "self-improvement circles." They created their own spaces to discuss literature, art, and philosophy. Eventually, as they began to trust one another more, these conversations turned political ... and the "girls" started to talk about their awful working conditions.

Some of them also wrote for the *Lowell Offering*, a literary magazine that was overseen by the factory owners but written by and for the workers. It was the first magazine in U.S. history to be wholly run by women. The magazine started off as a collection of personal poems and essays and fit well with the young workers' interests in art and philosophy. It was founded to emphasize the positive things about the mills, but that soon changed. Sarah was a contributor and early on, wrote an essay called "The Pleasures of Factory Work" that praised some aspects of her job. But as conditions inside the mills got worse, notes of dissatisfaction and even rebellion began to show up in the workers' writing. Some wrote about the difficulties of working in the mills, while others shared political views. A worker named Betsey Chamberlain wrote a passionate piece about her dreams of an eight-hour workday and equal wages for men and women (the factory owners probably weren't thrilled about that one). It didn't take long for Sarah to change her tune, too, and begin writing very different essays.

Betsey had had plenty of inspiration for her own essay, and as she spent more time at the factory, Sarah quickly learned the truth about their jobs. The mill girls' days were long, dusty, and loud. They would spend 12 to 14 hours standing in front of a screaming spinning machine or power loom, breathing in cotton fibers and the stench of oil lamps. Bloody accidents were common, and there were no such things as safety regulations. Workers often got caught in the machine and were left missing fingers or other limbs. Some were scalped when their long hair was yanked into the machines, leaving them in agonizing pain. Cotton dust filled the air and put workers at risk of developing serious lung diseases. There was no ventilation, either. Managers intentionally nailed the windows shut to keep the air thick and humid, which helped keep thread pliable. They didn't much care how unbearable it was for the workers, especially when the mills became boiling hot in the summer.

When the "girls" finally got to go home to their small apartments, there was barely time to eat and sleep before the work bell rang again. Their free time was still theirs, though there was precious little of it. Frustrated and beaten down by the horrible conditions, many of them left the mills altogether, and went back home to their families. They decided that a smaller, safer life at home was worth giving up on their own dream. By the 1840s, enough of the original mill girls had left that the factory owners began hiring Irish immigrant women instead. This was intentional, too. The bosses knew that these poor immigrant workers were desperate for jobs and would accept lower wages, since some money was better than nothing at all.

Things seemed to get worse and worse, and Sarah's positive view of her job soon curdled. She realized that the mills weren't an empowering new adventure but were instead a terrible grind. She saw how the factory owners did not care about how tired, ill, or uncomfortable they were. It seemed obvious that all they cared about were their own profits, so they kept cutting wages and forcing the workers to speed up production. Sarah's bosses thought they could get away with it, too. Because the mill workers were young women, the rich men who employed them assumed that they'd be too scared to stand up for themselves. Those men couldn't have been more wrong.

By 1844, Sarah had had enough. She began organizing her coworkers around what seemed like an almost impossible goal: the ten-hour workday. Betsey had dreamed of only eight, but to these workers, even 10 would have been a huge improvement. It seemed possible, too, since federal workers had won it in 1840 and skilled workers in various industries had done the same years earlier. The mill girls were still working up to 16 hours a day, and they were sick of it. That year, 15 young workers in Lowell—including Sarah—founded a labor organization called the Lowell Female Labor Reform Association. Their first meeting took place in December 1844 at the Anti-Slavery Hall in Lowell. It was organized as a chapter of the New England Workingmen's Association, and Sarah was elected as its first president. By 1845, the organization had gained 600 members, and they were determined to convince the

Massachusetts state legislature to pass a law shortening the workday to 10 hours. It was a big goal, and they knew they'd need to build power outside their own workplaces to get there. The mill girls connected with members of the New England Workingmen's Association and worked together to send petitions to the legislature.

Thanks to their efforts, Massachusetts launched a formal investigation into the working conditions in the Lowell mills. State Representative William Schouler, who was the publisher of the *Lowell Offering* before he ran for office, was called to lead the investigation committee. He knew very well how terrible things were for the mill girls, since he'd spent years reading their writings about it. In 1842, after he bought the *Lowell Offering*, the magazine stopped printing Sarah's writing. By then, she had become a fierce advocate for workers' rights, and Schouler thought it was a bad idea to give her a platform to spread her ideas. He was a friend to the factory owners, and Sarah's writing was a liability. It would've been hard to have picked a worse person to lead the committee.

The odds were stacked against them, but Sarah still stood up to publicly testify about how bad it was for her and her coworkers. Other young mill workers joined her on the stand, which must have been nerve-racking for them. At the time, it was very rare for women to testify in front of men—or speak in public at all—and these young women were speaking directly to powerful politicians who had never even seen the filthy guts of a factory. But they did it anyway and held firm to their message. Sarah and her coworkers were fighters, and they knew their cause was just. Unfortunately, the legislature ignored their pleas, and decided not to take any action against the mills. Schouler and his colleagues didn't care what a bunch of raggedy young women had to say and didn't want to risk upsetting the wealthy factory owners.

Sarah got back at them later, though, when Schouler was running for reelection to the Massachusetts House of Representatives in 1845. Women did not have the legal right to vote yet, so she and her coworkers couldn't vote against him themselves. But Sarah and the Lowell Female Labor Reform Association had gotten very good at getting their message across. They used all their energy to convince their male coworkers in Lowell to vote Schouler out. "As he is merely a corporation machine, or tool, we will use our best endeavors to keep him in the 'city of spindles,' where he belongs, and not to trouble Boston folks with him," they wrote at the time. He ended up losing his election. The mill girls had not yet won their fight for the ten-hour workday, but they certainly won their battle with William Schouler.

Sarah started writing again, too. On May 29, 1845, the New England Workingmen's Association launched a new magazine called the *Voice of Industry*. A young mechanic named William F. Young was its editor, but he quickly invited Sarah to join the publishing committee. She wrote essays aimed at women workers, and ran the Female Department of the magazine, which printed letters and other writings by mill girls. She became known for her fiery, inspiring words about the factory owners' hypocrisy and the mill system's failings. "Whenever I raise the point that it is immoral to shut us up in a room 12 hours a day in the most monotonous and tedious employment, I am told that we have come to the mills voluntarily and we can leave when we will. Voluntarily!" Sarah wrote in the *Voice of Industry*. "The whip which brings us to Lowell is necessity. We must have money; a father's debts are to be paid, an aged mother to be supported, a brother's ambition to be aided and so the factories are supplied. Is this to act from free will? Is this freedom? To my mind it is slavery."

She was also very critical of the *Lowell Offering*, which had survived but became very owner-friendly in the years since Schouler had forced her to stop writing for the magazine. In a Fourth of July speech, she called its then-editor Harriet Farley "a mouthpiece of the corporations." Farley was a former mill girl herself and did not appreciate the insult. Sarah refused to take back her words, and the two women kept up a public feud for years. Things had certainly come a long way from "The Pleasures of Factory Work" and Sarah had no interest in pretending to play nice with anyone who didn't appreciate the workers' struggle.

She spent two years as the president of the Lowell Female Labor Reform Association. During that same time, she was also an officer in the predominantly male New England Workingmen's Association, and was the vice president of the Lowell Union of Associationists. In early 1847, she left the Lowell Female Labor Reform Association after a series of disagreements over its direction. She also stopped writing for the *Voice of Industry* in late 1846, after clashing with its new male editor. He disagreed with her over the role women should take in publishing the magazine, saying that her writing was "too radical." Sarah had heard it all before: she was too loud, too passionate, and too determined. She had come a long way from those early days as a bright-eyed farm girl, and had spent nearly a decade fighting to improve conditions in Lowell's mills, take down greedy factory owners, and ease the pain of her fellow mill girls. It had been a grueling, tiring fight, and Sarah was ready to leave the mills behind and try something new. The factory owners were probably very happy to see her go.

Sarah was a labor pioneer in many ways, but no one would have been able to predict her next move. In 1846, she relocated to Springfield, Massachusetts, and became the nation's first female telegraph operator. The tabletop telegraph machines must have felt tiny compared to the massive power looms she was used to, and the relative quiet of her new office must have been a relief. However, Sarah found that this job came with an old problem: she was being paid a quarter as much as her male coworkers. By then, she was totally over the unequal treatment she'd received during her entire life as a worker and refused to put up with it for a minute longer. After making history in her new job, she quit.

Her later years brought a lot more movement. She briefly went back to Lowell to work in the mills again, then moved to Philadelphia, and also spent time in Brooklyn. In 1850, she made yet another big change. She married a Scottish man named James Durno, and they moved to Albany, New York. James worked as a homeopathic doctor, and they set up a patent medicine business. Patent medicines were big business during this era, despite the fact that they claimed to treat all kinds of diseases but rarely worked. Some people got rich by selling these medically dubious potions anyway, and the Durnos got in on the action by selling their own cold remedies. Unlike the grifters and hucksters who dominated the patent game, Sarah became a real physician. She focused on treating women and children and was especially interested in respiratory diseases. Helping women and children with their breathing problems must have taken her back to her days in the mills, with their hot, cotton-filled, non-ventilated air. She had probably spent years working alongside other young women with nagging coughs, scratchy throats, and bleary eyes. Some part of that memory must have stayed with her. No matter how far she traveled, Lowell was always in her heart.

After Sarah left the labor movement, she never gave up on the fight for justice. She became deeply invested in the struggles for women's rights and the abolition of slavery, and was also involved in antiwar activism and the prison reform movement. Sarah died in 1889 at the age of 83 and was buried beneath the rolling green hills of Philadelphia's Laurel Hill Cemetery. She did not live to see American workers win the eight-hour workday, which was not formally passed until 1938—over one hundred years after she first stepped foot in Lowell and walked through those Hamilton Manufacturing Company doors. But we wouldn't have gotten there without her.

Ben Fletcher
The Radical Dockworker
1890–1933

The first and most important duty is for all of us to prepare ourselves for the final chapter in the life of Capitalism.

Benjamin Harrison Fletcher was extremely well-known during his lifetime—famous, even!—but much of what we know about his early life is still a mystery. Like many poor and working-class people of his time, he did not keep a diary or detailed records, but the little that has been documented is fascinating. We know that he was born in Philadelphia on April 13, 1890, to Southern parents who had likely been born into slavery in Virginia. Like many other formerly enslaved Black people, Ben's parents moved north following Emancipation, and Philadelphia was a logical choice to make their new home. During that period, the city was a major hub for the maritime industry, with a busy waterfront full of ships, sailors, and dockworkers. Philadelphia had a reputation as a progressive place thanks to its large Quaker population, who vocally opposed slavery and promoted peace between different groups of people. Before and during the Civil

War, it was also an important stop on the Underground Railroad, the secret network of safe houses that many enslaved people used to escape to freedom. According to Dr. Peter Cole, who wrote an important biography called *Ben Fletcher: The Life and Times of a Black Wobbly*, by 1890, the city had become very diverse. Established communities of free Black people lived alongside newer immigrants from places like Ireland, Italy, and Eastern Europe. As a South Philadelphia native, Ben grew up in a neighborhood full of people of various races and ethnicities who spoke different languages. That experience would come in handy later on, after he got a little older and started working for a living.

When Ben Fletcher was a young man, he would not have had many employment options. It was not his fault. Though slavery had been abolished, the city remained segregated along racial, ethnic, and gendered lines, and many white employers refused to treat Black workers fairly. Even the most skilled or highly educated Black men were offered very few job opportunities outside of manual labor. Black women had little choice but to work in domestic service as cooks or housekeepers. When those employers did hire Black people, they gave them the toughest, dirtiest, and most difficult jobs. In Philadelphia, that meant working on the docks. Black workers had worked in the city's maritime industry since its colonial days, loading and unloading the same cargo ships that had crossed the Atlantic Ocean to bring them and their families to this country as captives, ships that then helped the U.S. rise as a major player in the global economy. By 1910, there were at least a thousand Black men working on Philadelphia's docks. Among them was young Ben Fletcher.

Ben spent his days hauling cargo on and off the huge ships that crowded the waterfront. It was hard, backbreaking work, and it quickly wore down the workers' bodies. After a couple of years, Ben decided that something needed to change. He and his coworkers weren't being treated right or being paid enough for their heavy labor. After all, they were men, not machines. By then, Ben had also become involved in politics, and he wanted to have more of a voice on the job. He had joined the Socialist Party of America as well as the Industrial Workers of the World, a labor union that had welcomed workers of every race and gender since it was formed in 1905 (one of its founders, Lucy Parsons, was a Black woman). The IWW's stance on racial equality was especially important to him, because so many other labor unions at that time were segregated or did not allow Black workers to join at all. Most of the organized labor movement was just as guilty of the deeply entrenched racism that made it so difficult for Black workers to find employment. Though Ben was a firm union supporter, he had no problem calling out their hypocrisy. As Ben wrote in a 1922 essay for *The Messenger*, an independent, pro-labor magazine run by Black labor organizer A. Philip Randolph, the mainstream U.S. labor movement's attitude towards Black workers "is replete with gross indifference and, excepting a few components, is a record of complete surrender before the color line.... Organized Labor for the most part, be it radical or conservative, thinks and acts in the terms of the White Race." He respected integrated unions like the United Mine Workers of America, the Amalgamated Textile Workers, and the IWW for organizing across racial lines, but he also believed that Black workers needed to start a "nationwide movement" to harness the power of their labor on their own terms. If the mainstream labor movement was not going to accept him and his fellow Black workers as equals, Ben figured they should start their own.

His message resonated with many of the people he spoke with, and as part of his own organizing work, he traveled up and down the East Coast talking to Black dockworkers in different cities. Sometimes he ran into trouble on these trips. White workers and police weren't always thrilled to hear a Black man preaching a message of Black worker power, and once, in Norfolk, Virginia, he had to quickly leave town to avoid being attacked.

The risks didn't slow him down, though. By 1912, Ben had already become a well-known and well-respected face among the thousands of dockworkers who kept Philadelphia moving. Black workers made up about half of the workforce, and Ben spoke directly to them at local IWW meetings and in the union's newspaper, *Solidarity*. He showed them how the problems that Black workers faced—the racism and exploitation that defined their working lives and the promise of uniting workers along industrial lines—were all connected, and why they needed to stand together to fight back against an unfair system. He saw the IWW as the only labor organization that could be trusted to treat Black workers fairly and to address their combined struggles under racism and capitalism. "[Industrial unionism] is the abolition movement of the 20th century," he wrote in a letter to the *Baltimore Afro-American* in 1920. "And if sufficient numbers of workers rally to its standard, complete industrial emancipation will be the heritage of all us workers and we will become disenthralled from the thralldom of the rich."

In 1913, during a strike of 4,000 workers that brought the docks to a standstill, both the IWW and the International Longshoremen's Association came to Philadelphia and gave the workers a choice: Which union did they want to join? Both unions could see how much power the dockworkers had built, and they wanted them as members. The IWW was independent, but the ILA was affiliated with the American Federation of Labor (AFL), a group that represented multiple unions. The AFL was much more conservative than the IWW in several important ways. At the time, the AFL tolerated open racism within its member unions, and allowed its affiliates to segregate their union locals (you can imagine how Ben felt about that!). In a vote, the workers decided to join the IWW, and formed the Local 8 branch of the IWW's Marine Transport Workers Industrial Union. In doing so, Local 8 became home to the IWW's largest group of Black members (who made up a third of Local 8's membership, along with Irish workers, and other European immigrants), as well as the union's most influential Black organizer: Ben Fletcher.

For the next 10 years, Local 8 would control Philadelphia's waterfront. It was also one of the strongest and most effective union locals in the IWW. The union operated without contracts, instead relying on the threat of strikes and walkouts to keep employers in line and win improvements in their wages, safety, and working conditions. Ben and his union brothers saw how bosses would use workers' differences to divide them and were determined to ensure that Local 8's members did not fall into their trap. Instead, Local 8 actively worked to create an environment of respect and understanding between Black and white workers by permanently integrating their own work crews. They prioritized a culture of fairness, making sure that both Black and white workers got a turn to lead their union meetings, putting on anti-racism talks, and organizing picnics and social events for members' families to get to know one another.

Ben himself would become well-known up and down the East Coast as a traveling organizer and speaker, venturing "as far south as Norfolk [VA] and as far north as Boston [MA]" as Professor Cole wrote. He spent a lot of time speaking with workers in Baltimore, another big port city with a large Black population, and signed up hundreds of new IWW members there. He also traveled to multiple IWW conventions in Chicago and made friends with legendary IWW organizers like Big Bill Haywood and Elizabeth Gurley Flynn, but always headed back home to Philadelphia whenever his fellow workers needed him.

Ben's mission to organize the nation's dockworkers was going well up until 1917, when the U.S. government decided to enter World War I. The conflict had already been raging overseas for several years before the Americans got involved. When the government started drafting young men into the military and sending them over to fight in Europe, anyone who opposed the war was painted as unpatriotic—or worse, a threat to national security. The IWW's members were split in their opinion of the war, so the union decided not to make any official statements about it. Instead, individual members were left to make up their own minds. While many of them were very much opposed to the war, others decided to join up and fight. The conflict became very personal for Ben and his family when Ben's younger brother Clarence joined the army. As his family waited anxiously for news, Clarence was sent to fight in France. Thankfully, he eventually returned in one piece.

Philadelphia's port was especially important to the war effort, and Local 8 decided not to go on any strikes while the war was on. Ben knew that it could be dangerous to openly oppose the war, so he urged coworkers to be publicly supportive. Hundreds of Local 8 members joined the military and bought "liberty bonds" to fund the war effort. But despite his best efforts to avoid rocking the boat, Ben was arrested on September 5, 1917, when the Department of Justice raided IWW offices across the country in a massive sweep. Out of those nearly 200 arrests, Fletcher was the only Black IWW member to be charged.

The raids were not random. In fact, the U.S. government had decided that the IWW had to be eradicated. Politicians feared that the union's anti-capitalist politics and insufficient support for the war could spread to more working-class people. The war machine demanded total submission. In 1917 and 1918, President Woodrow Wilson and Congress passed a pair of laws that made it much more difficult for anyone to publicly oppose the war. Basically, they made it illegal. The Espionage Act of 1917 and the Sedition Act of 1918 were broadly written in a way that allowed the government to limit free speech and use the new laws as an excuse to crack down on people whose progressive political views they disagreed with and saw as threatening: socialists, anarchists, and union members. President Wilson himself said that anyone who was "disloyal" to the war effort had "sacrificed their right to civil liberties" like free speech, freedom of the press, and free expression. As a result of these laws and the raids that followed, over 2,000 people were eventually arrested between 1917 and 1920 and imprisoned for a wide range of violations. Their charges were serious: conspiring to strike, interfering with the draft, mail fraud, and even espionage and sedition. It didn't matter whether they were guilty of their charges or not (and most of them weren't!). The district attorney for Philadelphia made the government's intentions clear when he described the September raids as having been done "very largely to put the IWW out of business." Imagine how scared the government must have been of their union to have worked *that* hard to crush them!

Ben Fletcher was one of 166 people—all IWW members—who were arrested on the same day. Their trial dragged on for four months, and while Ben—who was renowned for his wry sense of humor—did his best to keep his friends' spirits up, the result was devastating. Despite Local 8's peaceful reputation and lack of opposition to the war, Ben Fletcher was sentenced to 10 years in federal prison and fined $30,000 (roughly $467,000 in 2021 currency). He was only 28 years old, and the U.S. government had decided he was guilty of treason. As the sentencing was read out, he joked to his friend Big Bill Haywood, another IWW organizer who was among the defendants, "The judge has been using ungrammatical language. . . . His sentences are much too long!"

All joking aside, Ben was in a tough spot. He and 93 other IWW members were shipped off on a special "convict train" to the United State Penitentiary in Leavenworth, Kansas, which was then the largest and most notorious maximum-security prison in the country. Leavenworth, nicknamed "Hell's Forty Acres," had a terrifying reputation for cruelty and violence. During Ben's time there, he and his friends in the IWW were abused, neglected, and suffered from the prison's awful conditions. The FBI monitored all the political prisoners, including Ben, but he still managed to build relationships with other IWW members and Black activists outside the prison. He also sent letters to be published in *The Messenger*, ensuring that his voice could be heard even while he was locked away. While Ben and the others were stuck in Kansas, their friends outside the walls were raising money, launching appeals, and petitioning the government for their release. The end of WWI came on November 11, 1918. Once the dust cleared, the public began asking questions about all the people who'd been locked up during the war. Had all of those wartime arrests *really* been necessary? And if the war was over, why were they still imprisoned? Congress grudgingly repealed the Sedition Act in 1920, and a flood of political prisoners began to be released later that year.

Thanks to the efforts of his supporters throughout the country, Ben was released on bail in February of 1920. After taking a moment to catch his breath, he dove right back into his work with Local 8, who had badly missed his leadership and energy. He definitely hit the ground running. Later that year, he helped lead a huge strike of nearly 10,000 dockworkers in Philadelphia, using his people skills to convince multiple other unions to join Local 8 on the picket line. Over the next few years, Ben continued organizing, traveling, and giving speeches. In the 1930s, he got married to a nurse named Clara and moved to New York City. He set up an IWW office there and spoke out in support of striking coal miners in Harlan County, Kentucky. Those years of unjust imprisonment in one of the country's worst prisons had never broken him. If anything, it had made him even more determined to keep going. He refused to give up on his dreams of working-class power and multiracial solidarity.

Ben continued to play an active role in the IWW until 1933, when he suffered a serious stroke that sent his health into a sharp decline. That same year, as he wound down his incredible career as one of the IWW's most important organizers, President Franklin Delano Roosevelt finally pardoned him alongside many of his fellow IWW members who had been sent to prison over a decade earlier. As far as Ben was concerned, it was too little, too late. Instead of supporting his organizing work or listening to his message, the government had called him a traitor and thrown him in prison. Like so many other important Black activists before, during, and after his time, Ben Fletcher was punished for speaking up for his people—but history will remember him for what he was, a true working-class hero.

Ben died in 1949, and is buried in the Evergreens Cemetery in Brooklyn, New York. He had devoted his life to improving workers' lives and paid dearly for it. He weathered a storm, kept the faith, and laid the groundwork for the next century of struggle. And after all the hardships and setbacks, he never gave up. As he wrote in *The Messenger* in 1923, "It is to be hoped that in the near future, all labor will be united for one common cause. It is an undeniable fact that all labor has something in common: a desire for a higher standard of living. This can only be attained through interracial solidarity in the mixed union."

Clara Lemlich
The Fiery Garment Worker
1886–1982

I move that we go on a general strike!

Unless you were rich, New York City at the turn of the century was an awful place to live. It was an even worse place to work. By 1910, nearly 5 million people called the city's five boroughs home. (To put that in perspective, the country's second biggest city, Chicago, was only half that size!) Over 2 million humans were squeezed onto the island of Manhattan alone, which was also the heart of its industry and commerce. While the wealthy enjoyed airy mansions uptown, the city's working classes were stuck with the less desirable land by the river, where basic resources like sanitation were primitive at best. Disease and decay were rampant in these poorer neighborhoods, and the city's leaders seldom did much about it. There were no safety regulations, and the city health department was a joke. Working people's home lives were brutal, but their job conditions were even tougher: people were often injured or killed on the job, which put families deeper into poverty. Child labor was not only normal, it was also everywhere, even in the most dangerous factories.

Much of the city's workforce was made up of immigrants who had traveled to the U.S. in search of better lives. Instead, they were crowded into tiny apartments and expected to work long hours for pennies. Thousands of immigrant families made their home in the borough's Lower East Side, where life was hard but did have its joys. The area was a cultural melting pot, with immigrants from a variety of different places gathered to share food, music, art, and political ideas. Eastern European Jewish socialists, German communists, and Italian anarchists made friends with American trade unionists and Irish republicans, sharing ideologies, and building solidarity. Everyone was tired, dirty, poor, and miserable—but they still dreamed of building a better life and had lots of ideas about how to do it. This was the environment where Clara Lemlich grew up, and it had a huge impact on what she would decide to do with her future.

Clara was born in Gorodok, Ukraine, on March 28, 1886. Her family was Jewish, and she grew up speaking Yiddish. As a child, Clara longed to go to school, but none of the schools in her area would accept Jewish students. At the time, Ukraine was part of the Russian Empire, and the Russian government was extremely hostile toward Jewish people.

They were denied basic rights and opportunities and were treated as second-class citizens—or worse. For this reason, Clara's parents did not want her to learn the Russian language or read Russian literature; it was too painful for them to imagine their little girl speaking the language of their enemies. But Clara wanted to be educated, so she taught herself Russian anyway. She loved to read and as a teenager started working to be able to buy books. She sewed and wrote letters for her neighbors to afford books by writers like Leo Tolstoy and Karl Marx. Their revolutionary ideas about labor, capital, and equality burned in her young mind. When she closed her eyes and thought about what she'd learned, the world seemed bigger, bolder, brighter. She began to wonder—what if another life was possible?

When Clara was 17, her family decided to find out. Whatever else was out there had to be better than what was happening at home. The Russian government had become increasingly intolerant of the Jewish population, and Jewish villages were being targeted by horrifyingly violent anti-Jewish raids called pogroms. It was not safe for Clara or her loved ones anymore, so they left their home in 1903 and sailed across the ocean to New York City. When they arrived, they settled on the Lower East Side alongside a diverse array of other immigrant families. Only two weeks later, Clara was working in a garment factory with hundreds of other young immigrant women just like her. She would have preferred to keep reading and learning, but her family needed the extra money. Like so many other girls before her, she put down her books and went to work.

Clara landed on her feet because there was no other option—her family needed to eat, and everyone had to contribute to keep them going. She was tough, but it must have been an overwhelming experience for her to leave her village, cross the stormy sea on a massive ship, and then immediately enter the chaotic, colorful, confusing heart of New York City's working-class immigrant world. It was so different from her rural home and so much about it was scary, unfamiliar, and difficult, but still—it was safer than Ukraine, and it gave her family an opportunity to start over. Maybe New York City would be a place that would welcome Clara's passion for learning and hope for a fairer world. Maybe she could be something more.

Clara was just one of the thousands of young women who worked in the city's factories, shops, and markets. They lived similar lives, but their experiences were not universal among New York City's women. While rich women stayed home, depended on servants, and wouldn't have dreamed of dirtying their hands with actual labor, working-class women and girls had to work double shifts. First, they worked at home caring for their families, and then they had to clock in at a job, where they would be paid much less than their male coworkers. There was a racial difference, as well. In the early 1900s, New York City's population was mostly white, and just like in Philadelphia, its Black residents and residents of color were limited to a handful of professions. For Black women, that almost always meant working in domestic service for the rich white women who could afford to hire (and underpay) them. Working-class white women also worked as domestics, but more often they worked in laundries and in manufacturing, specifically the garment industry.

The garment factories were especially brutal. Many of those women spent their days in makeshift sweatshops. They would then take home piles of unfinished clothes (called piecework) to continue laboring over after they finished their factory shifts. Others worked 12-hour days in the factories themselves for as little as $3 per week. Just like the New England mill girls, working decades before them, thousands of women and girls had their limbs—or hair—caught in the machinery and lost both. Wages were low, and the workers were treated as expendable. Women were especially vulnerable to harassment and abuse from male factory bosses, and were constantly at risk of malnutrition, sleep deprivation, and disease. Some bosses liked to lock the factory doors in between shifts to prevent workers from stealing. Just as Sarah Bagley endured years earlier, these garment factories had no ventilation; they were freezing in winter and boiling hot in summer. Clara was appalled at the conditions and described the experience of working in a garment factory as "unbearable."

Unlike Sarah Bagley, Clara never thought of her factory job as fun or exciting. All she saw was how unfair it all was. "The bosses in the shops are hardly what you would call educated men, and the girls to them are part of the machines they are running," she once wrote. By 1905, two years after she'd set foot in New York City, she had begun organizing with the International Ladies' Garment Workers' Union (ILGWU). Garment workers knew they could trust her, because she was one of them; they shared the same dreary, sweaty job and lived in the same crowded neighborhood. Clara was a born leader, and her self-taught education in revolutionary ideas finally came in handy. As tensions increased between the workers and the factories, she got her first taste of collective action. Clara led her coworkers out on strikes in three different shops between 1906 and 1909. By 1909, she was on the union's executive board, and had become well-known among the city's workers for her fiery commitment to the cause.

She was not alone in the fight. In 1909, a group of other young Jewish women workers at Leiserson Company, the Rosen Brothers, and the Triangle Shirtwaist Factory, all garment manufacturers on the Lower East Side, decided that they'd had enough. Their bosses were making huge profits, but they were stuck in a cycle of bad pay and brutal workdays. It was time to fight back, and that September, they went on strike. Clara was working at the Leiserson Company at the time, and helped organize the workers as they got ready to walk. Each group had specific grievances with their employers, but their shared demands were for higher wages and safer working conditions. The Rosen Brothers quickly settled with their workers, but the other two companies refused to negotiate. Clara was arrested a total of 17 times on the picket line as the strike continued day after day outside the Leiserson factory. One night, company men followed her home and attacked her. They broke six of her ribs and left her bleeding in the street. She limped home and did her best to keep her injuries secret. (Clara never told her parents what she was doing because she didn't want to worry them, but it's hard to imagine how she explained away her bruises.)

As the dual strikes went on, a big meeting was called by the city's other garment workers to decide whether or not to join the Leiserson and Triangle workers. Speakers— most of them men—talked for hours about the pros and cons of the idea. They focused on the needs of male garment workers and were not interested in the women's struggle. The male leaders dismissed women workers as weak and thought that they were impossible to organize. Frustrated and fired up from weeks of picketing, Clara called out that she wanted to speak. The crowd made room for her five-foot self to take the stage. "I am a working girl," Lemlich cried out in Yiddish, the language that most of the women garment workers spoke. Her big voice immediately commanded the room's attention. "One of those who are on strike against intolerable conditions. I am tired of listening to speakers who talk in general terms. What we are here to decide is whether we shall or shall not strike. I offer a resolution that a general strike be declared—now!"

The crowd roared in agreement. The next morning, Clara and 15,000 of her fellow garment workers hit the streets. By the end of the day, there were 20,000 of them. By the end of the week, between 30,000 and 40,000 young women garment workers had walked off their jobs in a massive strike. The newspapers called it "The Revolt of the Girls," but the strike has gone down in history as the Uprising of the 20,000. The New York Women's Trade Union League (WTUL) provided financial support and offered to serve as the workers' representatives. When the strike finally ended in February, the WTUL had signed contracts with 339 out of 353 factories. The union contracts included new rules over safety standards, including shorter hours, fire safety, and handling of fabric scraps.

One notable holdout? The notoriously anti-union Triangle Shirtwaist Factory, whose owners, Max Blanck and Isaac Harris, refused to agree to any of the workers' demands. The men were known as the "Shirtwaist Kings" and ran the city's largest shirtwaist factory. They were former garment workers themselves and saw the strikes as a personal attack (think of them as a pair of suit-wearing versions of Harriet Farley, the mill worker–turned–union buster). They also saw the union as a threat to their business model, which relied on pushing workers to produce as much as possible as quickly as possible. If they slowed down to make things safer, they'd lose money—and that mattered more to them than the workers' safety. The factory owners responded to the strike by hiring police to arrest and sometimes violently attack the women. They were not unique there—remember Clara's broken ribs—but the Shirtwaist Kings were especially committed to breaking the union. For them, the fight was personal. They saw the workers as ungrateful traitors who were afraid of a little hard work, an opinion that showed just how much distance there was between them and the factory floor.

The garment industry strike went on for 11 weeks. As smaller shops quietly agreed to workers' demands, more workers at other shops would join in on the strike at their own workplaces. Clara played an important role, but was just one of many leaders. In one month alone, 723 people were arrested. The women workers threw themselves into the strike, giving speeches, raising strike funds, and holding meetings. Finally, the union's negotiating committee decided to call off the strike on February 15, 1910. It wasn't a total win, but it wasn't a defeat, either. Eighty-five percent of the shirtwaist makers in New York City joined the ILGWU, and Clara's union, ILGWU Local 25, added about 10,000 members. The 339 employers who signed contracts with the union agreed to a number of improvements.

The strike inspired a wave of labor actions across the country, but Blanck and Harris continued to refuse to recognize their workers' basic rights. Their stubbornness must have been frustrating for Clara and her friends at the time . . . but Blanck and Harris's uncaring attitude toward worker safety would also turn out to be one of the deadliest miscalculations in U.S. labor history.

March 25, 1911 started out just like any other day at the Triangle Shirtwaist Factory, which occupied the top three floors of the 10-story Asch Building in Manhattan's Greenwich Village. Since the factory's owners still refused to agree to a 52-hour workweek, about 600 people were still working there that Saturday afternoon. The women—most of them Eastern European Jewish and Italian immigrants—toiled away amidst dusty piles of fabric scraps, churning out shirtwaist after shirtwaist as the sunlight filtered in weakly through smudged windows. As usual, all the doors had been locked behind them as they'd trickled in for their shift. Two hundred of them were stationed on the top floor. Then around 4:45 p.m., a fire broke out.

It tore through the factory. With the doors locked, a slow, small elevator and a narrow fire escape on the side of the tall building offered the only chance to escape. That elevator soon broke down, making the fire escape the only option. Since Blanck and Harris had also refused to agree to the WTUL contract's new safety standards, fabric scraps piled around the sewing machines on the factory floor provided fuel for the fire. It took less than 30 minutes for the building to become a roaring inferno.

As the fire consumed everything—and everyone—in its path, horrified onlookers looked up at the building's windows. Dozens of young women crowded onto the rickety fire escape, desperate for an exit. When the fire brigade showed up, they were unable to offer any help; their ladders were too short to reach the factory's windows on the ninth floor. All they could do was watch as the women desperately searched for a way out and found only one. Soon after, the bodies began to fall.

"Up in the [ninth] floor girls were burning to death before our very eyes. . . . Down came the bodies in a shower, burning, smoking-flaming bodies, with disheveled hair trailing upward," William Shepherd, a United Press reporter who had witnessed the tragedy, later wrote.

"On the sidewalk lay heaps of broken bodies.... I looked upon the heap of dead bodies and I remembered these girls were the shirtwaist makers. I remembered their great strike of last year in which these same girls had demanded more sanitary conditions and more safety precautions in the shops. These dead bodies were the answer."

At the end of that terrible day, 146 workers had died. The panicked victims had been unable to escape the rising flames. Their young bodies were either broken on the sidewalk after jumping to their deaths or were suffocated by the billows of smoke inside the stuffy factory. Others were burned alive on the factory floor. Some were as young as 14. The next day, the corpses were placed in plain pine boxes and laid out in rows at the end of Manhattan's Charities Pier. The pier was also known as Misery Lane, as it served as a makeshift pop-up morgue whenever a disaster struck the city. Thousands of family members and onlookers streamed past, searching for familiar faces amidst the rows of burned and mangled bodies. They desperately looked for their daughters, wives, sweethearts, and sisters among the coffins. Some of the victims were never identified.

At the time, photography was still very new. When photos of the fire's victims hit the city's more than 30 newspapers the day after the blaze, New Yorkers reacted first with horror, and then with outrage. The images of these young women's tragic deaths chilled the nation and set into motion immediate efforts to reform the industry. In June 1911, the New York State Legislature's newly created Factory Investigating Commission sent inspectors into the city's tenements, factories, and sweatshops. Horrified by their findings, the commission passed 36 work safety laws in three years.

Following the tragedy, Blanck and Harris were arrested on first- and second-degree manslaughter charges. They hired a high-powered lawyer to represent them. Their lawyer argued that the owners had not known about the locked doors at the time of the fire—even though it was company policy to lock them each day. The two men were eventually acquitted of all charges. Worse, they turned a profit off it. Blanck and Harris were able to collect insurance money for the burned building and raked in $60,000, more than the fire had actually cost them in damages—about $400 per victim. In 1913, the pair reached a settlement with the victims' families, paying out one week's wages for each dead worker. Those payments came out to about $75 for each lost life.

Sadly, the owners did not learn their lesson. Later that year, Blanck was arrested again for locking a factory door during work hours, just as he'd done two years previously. He was later fined for a separate incident in which an inspector found flammable materials on the factory floor. In 1914, the pair were fined again for adding fake labels to the garments saying they'd been manufactured under "good workplace conditions." In 1918, the Triangle Shirtwaist Factory shuttered its doors for the final time and its owners walked away to live out the rest of their lives in comfort.

"I have always tears in my eyes when I think [of it]," Rose Freedman, the sole remaining survivor of the fire, said in a 2000 PBS documentary before her death at age 107 in 2021. "It should never have happened. The executives with a couple of steps could have opened the door. But they thought they were better than the working people. It's not fair because material, money, is more important here than everything. That's the biggest mistake—that a person doesn't count much when he hasn't got money. What good is a rich man and he hasn't got a heart?"

As for Clara, she was not present at the fire, though it's more than likely she knew many of its victims. She'd spent years organizing alongside the same young immigrant women who'd marched on the picket lines and labored on the factory floor. After the Uprising of the 20,000, she had been blacklisted from the garment industry. No factory would hire her, because they knew she would not let them get away with poor treatment. Instead, she worked as an organizer and political activist. She became very involved in the women's suffrage movement and continued to advocate for workers' rights. In 1913, she married Joe Shavelson, a printer and fellow labor activist. They had three children—Irving, Martha, and Rita—and moved to Brownsville, Brooklyn. She had come a long way from her childhood village, and that suited her just fine.

During the later chapters of her life, Clara continued to cause plenty of trouble. While she worked at home raising her three children, she also organized other mothers and housewives. In 1926, she joined the Communist Party and helped found the United Council of Working-Class Housewives. The organization supported the wives and families of striking workers by raising funds and providing food and childcare. As the years went on, the council expanded its focus to include issues of food prices, housing, and education. They also began working with other women's organizations to build a bigger coalition and changed their name to the Progressive Women's Councils. With Clara as their president, the women led rent strikes and protested rising food prices. In 1935, they led a boycott that shut down 4,500 New York City butcher shops that had been overcharging their working-class customers. The housewives' movement Clara helped create ultimately forced the government to lower food, utility, and housing prices, and laid the groundwork for modern consumer protection groups and tenants' unions.

During the 1940s, Clara returned to the labor movement

again. She served on the American Committee to Survey Trade Union Conditions in Europe and protested nuclear weapons as an organizer for the American League against War and Fascism. She had grown up, but had not left behind her days as one of the movement's *farbrente Yidishe meydlekh* (fiery Jewish girls). She was still regarded as dangerous, too. Thanks to her decades of activism and membership in the Communist Party, she and her family were surveilled by the U.S. government for over 20 years. In 1951, she was forced to testify before the House Committee on Un-American Activities. Undeterred, Clara kept organizing even after she officially retired from the ILGWU in 1954.

When she was 81, Clara moved into a Jewish nursing home in Los Angeles. Almost 80 years after she left home and became one of New York City's most respected labor icons, she found one more cause to fight for. Before she passed away at the age of 96 on July 12, 1982, she helped the nursing home staff organize a union.

Frances Perkins
Giving Workers a Fair New Deal
1880-1952

Without action, ideas are powerless.

Most of man's problems upon this planet, in the long history of the race, have been met and solved either partially or as a whole by experiment based on common sense and carried out with courage."

Fannie Coraline had never been all that attached to her name. She'd always been a studious, independent sort of person, even as a little girl growing up in Massachusetts. After she'd finished college and moved out of her parents' house, "Fannie" began to sound childish. It didn't fit her anymore, and neither did a lot of things about her comfortable, conservative upbringing. Her parents had been loving but strict, and she had to keep her individuality under wraps as long as she lived at home. When the opportunity finally came for her to make a change, she didn't blink—and became Frances. It was a small decision that would have a major impact on the world. She may have been born Fannie, but the shopkeeper's daughter could have never predicted just how many people would eventually come to know the name Frances Perkins.

Frances had been born in Boston on April 10, 1880. She grew up in Worcester and spent her summers with her grandparents on the family farm in Newcastle, Maine. They were an old New England family who could trace their roots back past the Revolutionary War, and were deeply proud of their history. Her father ran a paper store, and both parents kept a close eye on Frances and her sister. Frances grew into a bright, curious little girl who loved to read. Though they were religious and conservative, her parents encouraged her interest in education. Her father taught her to read Greek when she was eight years old, and she dove into classical literature. Frances also became invested in the fight against injustice at a young age, when she first saw the impact of poverty on some of her classmates at school. "I had to do something about unnecessary hazards to life, unnecessary poverty," she once wrote. She felt a responsibility to act. "It was sort of up to me."

It was a given that Frances would continue her education, even though most girls in her position would have stopped much earlier. During that era, it was not at all common for girls to go to college. They were encouraged to learn just enough to make them good wives and mothers, then to stay home with their families. Frances wasn't interested in taking that path, so her parents agreed to send her to Mount Holyoke, a women's college not far from their home in Worcester. She thrived in the academic environment, and her teachers encouraged her to take difficult courses in chemistry and physics. Each challenge felt like a new adventure, and Frances was truly in her element.

At Holyoke, she also got a political education both inside and outside the classroom. She was deeply inspired by a speech from Florence Kelley, the executive secretary of the National Consumers League, who showed her that it was possible to make a career out of helping people in need. And a class on American economic history taught by historian Annah May Soule intensified her interest in poverty and injustice. She and her classmates were given an assignment to visit local factories to interview workers and see what kind of conditions they were working in. What she found there shocked and upset her. The dirty, dangerous factories were much different from her family farm or her father's tidy store. "There were absolutely no effective laws that regulated the number of hours they were permitted to work," she later wrote. "There were no provisions which guarded their health nor adequately looked after their compensation in case of injury. Those things seemed very wrong. I was young and was inspired with the idea of reforming, or at least doing what I could, to help change those abuses."

At the same time, Frances also became involved in the women's suffrage movement, and dedicated herself to the cause of winning women the right to vote. In 1901, Frances's senior year of college, Florence Kelley, the executive secretary of the National Consumers League, came to speak. Kelley was a suffragist too and was committed to helping consumers understand how their choices impacted workers. She spoke about the evils of child labor and sweatshops. Frances listened closely, thinking about the faces of the factory workers she'd interviewed. She was starting to get an idea. Maybe there was something she could do to help.

After graduation, her parents decided it was time for Frances to come back home. Maybe she could find part-time work as a teacher, they thought, and spend the rest of her time at the family home until she found a nice young man to marry. As they saw it, they'd indulged her hunger for education long enough; it was time to act like a proper young lady. Instead, Frances waved goodbye to her shocked family, and moved to bustling New York City to find a job as a social worker.

Her goal was to help the poor and working people who she'd been worrying about since she was little, but a big heart wasn't the only qualification she needed for such a demanding profession. Her Greek and chemistry classes weren't quite as practical as they'd seemed back when she was in college—or at least, the social work agencies she visited weren't very impressed. She had no practical experience in the field yet, so it proved impossible to find a job. Deflated, Frances went back home to Massachusetts to think about her next step. She wouldn't be the first (or the last) new college grad to have to move back in with her parents, but Frances wasn't planning on staying very long. Her college education made it possible to pick up teaching jobs around Boston, but that got old, fast. Nothing felt quite right.

In 1904, she moved to Chicago. There, she worked as a science teacher at a private academy. In her free time and on vacations, she volunteered at Hull House, a settlement house founded by progressive activist Jane Addams to serve poor citizens and recently arrived European immigrants. It offered job training, childcare, language lessons, and food assistance. It had taken a few tries, but Frances was finally doing what she wanted to do—helping the people who needed it most. She had learned a lot in college, but this was a whole new kind of education. She connected with workers and their families. She heard stories about workplace abuse and saw families struggle to survive. Meanwhile, the wealthy prospered. It became clear to Frances that something was very, very wrong. That was also around the same time that she joined a new church and officially changed her name from Fannie to Frances.

It was her way of saying to the world, "This is who I am. I am independent, and my life is my own."

To her frustration, her teaching job kept Frances from fully committing to social work. She was finally starting to gain enough experience working at Hull House to qualify for a full-time job as a social worker, but her teaching job took up far too much time. She felt stuck, but knew that she was not meant to be a teacher. It gave her an opportunity to teach a new generation of youngsters about the world, but Frances wanted to be out there making change herself, not reading about other people's successes in a textbook.

In 1907, she moved again, and began working at an organization in Philadelphia helping vulnerable immigrant women and girls. Eager to learn as much as she could, she used her free hours in the city to take classes in sociology and economics at the University of Pennsylvania. Years of working directly with poor and working-class people had already been the best education imaginable, but diving deeper into her chosen subjects only added to her conviction that she'd found her calling. Frances might not have wanted to be a teacher anymore, but she was still an excellent student. A year later, she got an opportunity to move to New York City to study political science at Columbia University. Her first trip to the city had been unsuccessful—but now, Frances was ready to take another bite out of the Big Apple.

The National Consumers League needed someone to run their New York City office, and—what joy!—Frances got the job. Her work there focused on several areas, including child labor, poor wages and hours for women workers, and workplace fire hazards. She reconnected with Florence Kelley, the woman who had given her so much hope as a college student, and they became close friends. Her hard-won social work background was essential for the job, but Frances also had to navigate working with the government. The League wanted New York to pass a bill limiting women workers to 54 hours per week, so Frances had to make friends with politicians and lobby them for support. She became close with two ambitious young politicians: Theodore Roosevelt and his cousin Franklin D. Roosevelt. They and the others she spoke with were all men; women still did not even have the right to vote. It was a difficult campaign, and despite their best efforts, the League's bill failed. Too many of the male politicians had ignored their message, so Frances knew she would have to find other ways to make them listen.

Frances still made time for fun when she could, though. One sunny day in 1911, Frances was visiting friends in Greenwich Village. The neighborhood was full of artists, musicians, and political activists, and open-minded young people like her and her friends loved its lively atmosphere. It was usually a delightful place to spend an afternoon.

However, that day, something was wrong. As she and her friends sipped their tea, she heard people outside yelling about a fire. She peeked outside and saw smoke pouring out of a big building nearby. Frances ran over to investigate, and unexpectedly became a witness to a horrible tragedy.

The Triangle Shirtwaist Factory was on fire, and 146 workers were trapped inside. Frances knew all about the kind of workplace fire hazards inside too many garment factories, so she could guess what had happened. The lives lost that day weighed on her even more because she knew how preventable it had all been. She later said that the fire was a "never-to-be-forgotten reminder of why I had to spend my life fighting conditions that could permit such a tragedy."

Frances was 31 then and had long assumed her adult life would revolve around volunteer social work and family commitments. But she couldn't unsee the factory fire, or get the workers' screams out of her mind. Her years of experience working with other young immigrant women just like them meant that she could picture exactly what their lives had been like, and feel the devastation of their families. Frances knew she needed to act and got her chance when her pal Theodore Roosevelt recommended her for the Committee on Safety in the City of New York. The committee was formed after the Triangle Factory

Fire to investigate factory safety. She left her job at the National Consumers League and started leading factory inspections. She also advocated for legislation to protect workers, shorten the hours they had to work, and to create a minimum wage. In 1913, New York finally passed the 54-hour bill Frances had been pushing for years and crossed off another win on her ambitious to-do list.

That same year, Frances married an economist named Paul Caldwell Wilson, who worked for the Bureau of Municipal Research in New York. Some people were shocked when she chose to keep her own name instead of taking his, but names were important to Frances; she'd chosen her own once already, and it was working out just fine, thank you! They had a daughter, Susanna, in 1916, when Frances was 36. Their family life became more complicated when Susanna was still little, and Paul began to struggle with mental illness. Ultimately, he spent much of their marriage in and out of hospitals, while Frances supported the family financially. She kept her personal life private, but later in her life, Frances had very close relationships with women, including fellow activist Mary Harriman Rumsey and New York congresswoman Caroline O'Day.

Work was Frances's main focus. When Al Smith, a close friend of hers, was elected governor in 1918, he invited Frances to join the New York State Industrial

Commission. Her job was to make sure that the new health and safety laws were being followed. Obviously, this was right up her alley, and she ended up working there for the next 10 years. Then, in 1929, after her old friend Franklin D. Roosevelt was elected governor, he made her the New York state industrial commissioner. It was now her job to run the entire state's labor department. This was a big promotion, and there was a *lot* to do. Even an overachiever like Frances would've probably been a little intimidated—and the timing couldn't have been worse. Unemployment was rising, and the state was scrambling to keep up. That year, a stock market crash began an economic crisis that would launch the U.S. into the Great Depression. Millions of people lost their jobs and were thrown into poverty. As the head of the state labor department, it was up to Frances to come up with some kind of plan to help. She'd been interested in the idea of unemployment insurance—temporary income for workers who have lost their jobs—and traveled to the U.K. to learn how their system worked. When she came back, she had the blueprints for another one of her big ideas.

In 1932, as the Depression continued to squeeze the country, Franklin D. Roosevelt was elected president. One of his first actions was to ask Frances to be the secretary of labor. She would be the first woman to serve in a presidential cabinet as well as the first person to hold that job title. It was a huge honor, but when Roosevelt called her with the job offer, she told him that he would need to agree to a few things first. She outlined her major priorities, and said that if he wouldn't support them, she was out. The job would not be worth her time if she couldn't actually get things done.

Her wish list included the implementation of a 40-hour workweek for all workers, as well as a minimum wage, the abolition of child labor, unemployment compensation, Social Security, stronger safety regulations, and universal health insurance. These were all very ambitious ideas, but she knew how necessary they were for the country's workers to survive, thrive, and succeed. Roosevelt agreed, and she accepted his offer to join him in the White House. Frances immediately put all of her years of experience on the ground and in local politics to use, and thanked her lucky stars for all of the adventures and wrong turns she'd taken that had led her here. She would spend 12 years leading the Labor Department, longer than any other secretary of labor. And, Frances being Frances, she got a *lot* done in those 12 years!

The biggest achievement of Roosevelt's presidency was a series of social, economic, and political reforms and programs called the New Deal. Though she seldom gets the credit for it that she deserves, Frances played a huge role in shaping that legislation. She was later quoted as saying that the New Deal began on March 25, 1911, the day of the devastating Triangle Shirtwaist Factory fire. Her work on the New Deal transformed the country and improved the lives of countless people by giving them an economic boost and strengthening their rights as workers. She helped draft the National Labor Relations Act, which created a National Labor Relations Board and made it easier for workers to organize unions. She was also behind the Fair Labor Standards Act of 1938, which established a minimum wage and prohibited child labor in many workplaces.

Frances was also involved in many different projects, including ones aimed at reducing unemployment, but her own biggest win was the passage of the Social Security Act. The final version of the Social Security Act was not as strong as Frances had hoped because of changes added by congresspeople (and lobbyists). She did not get universal health insurance—a demand that many people in this country are still trying to win. But the program, which provides for the health needs of disabled people, elderly people, people who were injured at work, and people who lose their spouses or parents, created an economic safety net. To this day, Social Security is a lifeline for millions of vulnerable people in the U.S. and remains one of the most popular government programs of all time.

During this period, the Labor Department also oversaw immigration and kept track of immigrant workers. As a result, Frances and her staff had to keep a close eye on global political events. They watched in horror as Nazi dictator Adolf Hitler rose to power in Germany in 1933 and began targeting the country's Jewish population for horrible mistreatment. In an effort to protect them from Hitler's evil plans, Frances ordered the department to help European Jewish refugees find safety in the U.S. Roosevelt did not want to relax the country's strict immigration laws, but Frances refused to stand down. It was a matter of life and death, and she knew that it was her duty to do everything she could to save as many lives as possible. Unfortunately, not everyone shared her views. She was often the lone voice standing against her government colleagues' anti-Jewish, anti-immigrant prejudices. To get around government opposition, she got creative and found legal loopholes to achieve her goals. By 1937, she had arranged for the safe passage of nearly 300,000 temporary and permanent refugees to the United States. She did not care if people criticized her. She knew it was the right thing to do.

As the years went by, Frances achieved more and more of her original goals and kept ticking things off her checklist. Congress often tried to stand in her way, but she was good at getting things done. The immigration fight had taught her how to work the system to her advantage, and how to handle negative backlash from her peers. Her years navigating New York state politics came in handy, as did her overall fearlessness. It was hard work, but she knew it was worth it. Her priority was always whatever was best for the workers. If anyone had a problem with that—so what!

Not everyone in the government liked Frances. They thought she was too radical, especially for a woman, and some government leaders disliked her pro-union stance. In 1939, Congress tried to impeach her over her support for a powerful union leader who had caused their allies in the business world one too many headaches. In 1934, Harry Bridges, an Australian longshoreman and labor leader who was living legally in the U.S., had helped organize a massive longshoreman's strike in San Francisco. It had shut down the city's ports for 83 days, and Congress was furious about it. They wanted to deport Bridges, but Frances pushed back, and did what she could to slow them down. Bridges ultimately stayed put, and so did Frances.

There was never a dull moment during Frances's time in the White House, and it came to an end just as unexpectedly it had started. On April 12, 1945, her friend Franklin Delano Roosevelt died a few months after being sworn in for his fourth term as president. His successor, Harry Truman, quickly took office and began cleaning house. Frances was much more progressive than Truman and could see the writing on the wall. Still mourning her former boss, she resigned from the cabinet a few weeks later. Frances and Roosevelt had known each other for over 35 years and built their careers together on their shared principles and goals. She went on to write a book about him called *The Roosevelt I Knew*, which is still regarded as one of the best biographies of FDR to date.

While her time in the White House was over, Frances was not ready to give up her career in public service. Truman respected her even though they disagreed on many matters, and he appointed her to the United States Civil Service Commission. She worked there for seven years dealing with employment discrimination and overseeing working conditions for civil servants. In 1952, her husband Paul died, and she left the agency. She was 72 years old, and for her final act, Frances decided to go back to her roots.

After a lifetime on the front lines of workers' rights, Frances became a teacher again. She had come full circle in a way. But this time, instead of trying to get bored private-school kids interested in science class, she went to teach at Cornell University's School of Industrial and Labor Relations. Sharing her wisdom with a new generation of labor activists and union leaders was much more her speed, and she also gave lectures at other universities about labor and economics. She kept at it until 1965.

That year, she died of a stroke at the age of 85 and was buried in her beloved Newcastle, Maine. She had kept the promise she had made back in 1911 to spend the rest of her life fighting for workers' rights and safety.

While her name isn't quite as well-known as that of the president she served alongside, the progress Frances made on behalf of the country's working class has changed millions of lives for the better. The woman behind the New Deal was a feminist and a self-proclaimed "revolutionist" who fought for what was right even when it was unpopular. "I came to Washington to work for God, FDR, and the millions of forgotten, plain common workingmen," she said of her time in government. And that is exactly what she did.

Lucy Parsons
The Fierce Revolutionary
1851–1942

Strike not for a few cents more an hour, because the price of living will be raised faster still, but strike for all you earn, be content with nothing less.

The 19th century allowed very little room for women of color to find their voices, let alone share them with the masses. The few who managed to break their silence often became figures of mixed curiosity and revulsion. When a young Black woman named Lucia Carter first entered the public eye, it wasn't on purpose. The town gossips in Waco, Texas, just had a lot to say about her relationship with an older fellow named Oliver, and after she met her husband, Albert, their tongues started wagging even harder. Little did they know that their small-town drama was destined to be the least interesting thing about Lucia—or Lucy—and her incredible, revolutionary life.

After Lucy left Waco, she would take on many roles and identities, and become an expert at adaptation. She was a chameleon, and her looks were a powerful tool. A tall, striking woman with strong bone structure, "copper" skin, dark eyes, and glossy black hair, she wore many faces. Lucy spent her life alternately claiming that her ethnic background was Spanish, Mexican, Indigenous, or some combination thereof. In reality, she was born in 1851 to an enslaved Black woman named Charlotte on a plantation in Virginia. Its white owner, Thomas J. Taliaferro, was thought to be her father. Lucy was 14 when the Emancipation Proclamation was signed, and she and her family were set free. Everything changed for them then, but for Lucy most of all. Her light skin would give her access to spaces that her darker-skinned mother and siblings would never see, and open up possibilities that were never available to most people with her background.

All of that would come later, though. First, the family moved to Texas, and settled down in Waco. When she was 21, Lucia met a white former Confederate soldier named Albert Parsons, who was working as a newspaper editor in town. She told him her name was Lucy, and from then on, it was. They fell deeply in love and decided to get married in 1872. There was just one problem, though: their union was only legal for a year. The Texas law that allowed people of color and white people to marry one another changed in 1873, and the young couple had to quickly leave Texas to avoid being arrested. They went north to Chicago, where the Parsonses settled in a lively German immigrant neighborhood. It was a world away from

Lucy's old ranch, and she became immersed in new and exciting radical political ideas.

She hadn't been very political before she met Albert, but together, they envisioned a world of true freedom and equality. They were drawn to anarchism, a political belief that the best way to fix society's problems is to burn it down and start all over again without any oppression or hierarchies. Anarchists wanted to create a new way of living, without a capitalist system to exploit people or a government to tell people how to live their lives. That all sounded pretty good to Lucy and Albert, who came from two very different backgrounds but arrived at the same conclusion. For someone like Lucy, who spent her early years as an enslaved worker with no control over her time or body, the idea of a society built on equality, liberty, and joy sounded like a beautiful dream. Together, the young couple hoped to make that dream a reality.

Chicago was a hot spot for the labor movement, and political people of all stripes got involved with the cause. Lucy and Albert soon became involved in the fight for an eight-hour workday, joining in a long struggle that had begun decades before either of them got there. Lucy was working as a dressmaker and knew all about long hours and hard work. In 1878, she joined the Chicago Working Women's Union, which gave Lucy her first experience with labor organizing. She also began to write political essays and worked to find her own voice. It was an excellent time for a passionate young writer to get published, because there were many daily newspapers and magazines that catered to workers and political radicals alike. It didn't hurt that Lucy's husband Albert was involved with the typing workers' union and was a writer himself. If she had something to say, there would be no problem getting it out in front of people.

This marked the beginning of a prolific writing career that spanned essays, editorials, fiction, and journalism. She became well-known for her take-no-prisoners writing style and workers appreciated how harshly she spoke against the ruling class. Word spread of this fascinating new writer, and soon, Lucy was being asked to speak at meetings and rallies. It was both difficult and dangerous for someone like her to speak publicly, but Lucy would embrace the challenge—and make it her trademark.

Lucy regularly held union meetings at her home and went to gatherings of workers throughout the city. She also used her dressmaking shop as a space for workers and labor organizers to congregate without attracting their bosses' attention. However, Lucy realized that her voice rang loudest in print and at the podium. She decided that harnessing that power as a public figure was the most effective way to advance the causes of labor and anarchism. She liked the attention and knew her words were powerful. It was certainly more interesting than sitting through yet another union meeting, and Lucy wanted to be where the action was. All the world was a stage for the "Goddess of Anarchy," as the newspapers called her, and she intended to explode onto it.

Audiences were thrilled by her sophisticated oratory skills, blistering anti-capitalist rhetoric, and appearance. Reporters regularly mentioned her brown skin and wrote about her beauty in their articles, which only added to her mystique. It was still rare to see any woman speaking publicly at that time, so it was extraordinary to see a woman of color like Lucy confidently take the stage and proceed to preach fire, brimstone, and anarchy to halls full of rowdy white male factory workers.

Lucy and Albert were also both involved with the Chicago chapters of the Knights of Labor, the first mass working-class organization in the U.S. The Knights were founded in 1869 as a secret society, but the organization grew in leaps and bounds under the watchful eye of founder Uriah Stephens. Membership numbers were high, as thousands of disgruntled workers seized on what seemed like the first chance they had to actually force some change. The Knights also cast a broad net. They organized workers who were "skilled" (those who were trained in a specific craft or trade, like carpenters or shoemakers) as well as "unskilled" laborers who entered the workforce without specific training, like the thousands who poured into factories as the Industrial Revolution heated up.

In 1883, the Knights became the first national labor organization to accept women and Black members, which was a big deal at a time when most other unions defaulted to racial segregation and discrimination. (They organized across religious lines as well, successfully bringing together groups of Catholic and Protestant Irish workers.) At the height of their influence, the Knights boasted nearly a million members, including Lucy and Albert. Unfortunately, by the end of the 19th century, the organization crumbled under the pressures of state suppression and competition from other unions. The final blow came from the violence and chaos around what would become known as the 1886 Haymarket Affair, which would also define the rest of Lucy's and Albert's lives.

On May 1, 1886, a large group of Chicago workers went on strike in support of the eight-hour workday. As part of the day's events, Lucy, Albert, and their young children led a march to support the workers; it would later become known as the nation's first May Day parade. Several days later, on May 4, people gathered in Chicago's Haymarket Square for a rally in support of strikers at the nearby McCormick Reaper Works. The workers who were on strike had been viciously attacked by police the day before. Among the speakers were Lucy's husband, Albert, and their friends August Spies and Samuel Fielden. All three men were steadfast advocates for the eight-hour-day movement that had been gathering momentum among the city's workers. They were also anarchists with deep ties to the city's organized labor community. Lucy wasn't the only public speaker in the family; Albert was also a popular speaker at rallies and had a habit of calling for violence during his speeches. He was a small, dapper man who didn't look like much of a fighter, but just like Lucy, his words struck terror into the hearts of the ruling class. On that day, though, his remarks were pretty restrained; he didn't even mention dynamite, which was one of his favorite oratory moves. As he ended his speech, the skies opened up and it began to rain. Since Lucy had their two children with her, they all rushed into a nearby saloon to dry off.

Samuel was up next, and as he was finishing his speech, police arrived to break up the rally. All of a sudden, a bomb was thrown into their path. The cops panicked and began firing wildly into the crowd. In less than five minutes, the square was empty. Eleven people were dead, and over 70 had been injured in the melee. Albert, Samuel, and August were all arrested alongside their fellow anarchists Adolph Fischer, George Engel, Michael Schwab, Oscar Neebe, and Louis Lingg. Many of the men contributed to the same newspapers as Lucy. They were radicals, organizers, and sometimes troublemakers, but there was no firm evidence connecting any of the men to the bombing. That didn't matter to the police or the local judiciary, who hated and feared their ideology and their support for the strikers. The eight men were all blamed for inciting a riot and tried as accessories to murder for the policemen who'd been killed during the confusion. One cop who'd been present told a reporter, "A very large number of the police were wounded by each other's revolvers," but that point didn't seem to matter, either. Lucy was only spared because she was a woman. Her speeches and essays had been just as vitriolic and wild as the men's had been, but the police apparently still believed that she didn't have the guts or motivation to be involved in such a dangerous plot. Their sexism saved Lucy from a lot of trouble, but not from the tragedy that was to come.

When it came time for the men to go to trial, an openly hostile judge and jury made it clear that they wouldn't be getting anything resembling fairness. Newspapers and politicians had been stirring up the public with horror stories about these allegedly evil, violent anarchists, and no one was on their side. Their fate was sealed before they even got a chance to argue, and all eight were declared guilty. Neebe was sentenced to 15 years in prison, and the other seven were sentenced to death. After months of appeals, Schwab's and Fielden's sentences were commuted to life in prison. Lingg took his own life in his prison cell. The rest—Engel, Fischer, Parsons, and Spies—were sent to the gallows on November 11, 1887. In the moment before he was killed, Spies cried out, "The time will come when our silence will be more powerful than the voices you strangle today." Those last words proved to be prophetic. In death, the Haymarket Martyrs' sacrifice shocked the world, and continues to echo through history.

Lucy was shattered. Police had prevented her from entering the prison to say one last goodbye to her beloved husband, and now he was gone. After Albert was first imprisoned, she had spent months crisscrossing the country to rally public support in their favor. She hoped to overturn the sentence, and fundraised money for his legal appeal. After his death, she was transformed into the Widow Parsons, a heavy burden she would carry until her own death many years later. For the rest of her life, Lucy devoted herself to keeping the memory of her husband and the Haymarket Martyrs alive. She never gave up on the cause of the working-class revolution, but the light went out of her life. All the words in the world hadn't saved Albert, and now she was left to continue the fight on her own.

The Haymarket Affair tore the labor movement and Chicago's anarchist community apart. Some people sympathized with the dead men and their supporters, but others blamed them for giving organized labor a bad name and hurting the eight-hour day campaign. Lucy struggled to find a new political home. In 1905, when she was invited to appear at the founding convention of a new union called the Industrial Workers of the World, she thought she'd found it. The IWW remains one of the most unique labor unions to have ever existed in the U.S. Its founding coalition of anarchists, socialists, Marxists, and trade unionists had a simple goal in mind: to organize all workers into one big union. The IWW wanted to uplift the working class, seize the means of production, and free themselves from the capitalist wage system. (You can see why Lucy was interested!)

That first convention featured a star-studded lineup of some of the 20th century's most influential labor activists, like the Western Federation of Miners's Big Bill Haywood and Vincent Saint John, American Railway Union president Eugene V. Debs, and United Mine Workers organizer Mary "Mother" Harris Jones. Along with Mary, Lucy was one of the only two women directly involved in the founding of the IWW. She had high hopes for the new organization, but to her frustration, she found that the other founders saw her as more of a mascot than an equal participant. She was just a famous face with a tragic story, not the powerful writer and organizer that she was. That didn't matter; she was going to be heard anyway.

Lucy used her position in the union to push for a stronger focus on working women and children. She also founded and edited *The Liberator*, an IWW-affiliated magazine that criticized capitalist exploitation and advanced the union's cause of free speech.

Lucy was a study in contradictions, many of them of her own creation. The image of herself she shared with other people acted as a suit of armor to keep her safe. Even while she was onstage calling for a bloody revolution, she tried to project the image of the perfect Victorian wife and mother. Her identity as one of the best-known anarchists in America clashed with her later involvement in the Communist Party. She focused her energies solely on white factory workers, dismissing or outright ignoring the labor struggles of Black workers in the South as well as in her own adopted home of Chicago. They certainly could have benefited from her talents for publicity, but her refusal to acknowledge her own Blackness separated her from her own community. It may have made it easier for her to find success within predominantly white spaces, but it also separated her from her roots, her painful memories of slavery, and what could have been her community.

The ugliest chapter in her history concerns her horrific treatment of her son, Albert Jr., who was with her and Albert on the day of the Haymarket bombing and walked behind his father's coffin with her. After the young man tried to enlist in the military during the Spanish-American War, Lucy stepped in and had him confined in a psychiatric institution. She had decided that his desire to serve was a sign of insanity and refused to allow him to follow his own convictions. He spent the rest of his life at the Elgin Asylum and died there in 1919. It's difficult to understand how she could have done such a terrible thing, but she never left an explanation.

Lucy always kept her armor on, even with her own family. It was as if she was allergic to showing any sign of weakness. Did she fear what might happen if she was her authentic self? She lived during an era when women were seen as inherently lesser than men and Black people were barely seen as human, so the risks were very real. Crowds cheered for her when she was "a Spanish maiden," but would they have welcomed her words so readily if they knew about her real background? Perhaps something from her earlier life told her not to risk it. In one of her few instances of accurate official recordkeeping, Lucy's children with Albert—Albert Jr. and Lulu—were marked Black on their birth certificates. Rumors about her true identity swirled throughout her life, and even appeared in the newspapers that reported on her actions. Still, the most famous Black women of her time refused to tell the world who she really was. As she told a nosy reporter in 1887, "The public have no right to my past. I amount to nothing to the world and people care nothing for me. I am simply battling for a principle." That principle changed in name over the years, but always boiled down to a simple dream: freedom, whatever that looked like to her.

Parsons took her secret to the grave. She continued to speak up for workers' rights well into her 80s, and died in a house fire on March 7, 1942, not long after the FBI had raided her library and burned her personal papers. It was as if they thought that even the memory of Lucy was too dangerous to keep alive.

While her name may have faded out of mainstream history, the work she did survived. No matter how complex Lucy was as a person, it's impossible to say that many of her actions didn't make a positive difference. She had a huge presence in the campaign for the eight-hour day. She founded or cofounded a half dozen labor organizations (including several that still exist, like the IWW and the International Ladies' Garment Workers' Union). She helped spread the idea of anarchism to the masses and invited people to share her utopian vision of the future. She rallied striking workers and educated the public on the plight of the working people and the capitalist greed bleeding them dry. She was especially fired up about the evils of child labor, frequently railing against the practice in her editorials and speeches. Remember, for Lucy, the topic of child labor was deeply personal. Unlike so many of her contemporaries in the labor movement and in Chicago's activist community, she had spent the first 12 years of her life working in a white man's house as an enslaved person.

As a formerly enslaved Black woman activist who took on the state and refused to be silenced, she had to work three times as hard to get as far as she did. But she did it anyway because *that's* who Lucy Parsons was.

Mother Jones
The Miners' Angel
1837–1930

Pray for the dead and fight like hell for the living!

Some people discover their life's purpose when they are very young. (You've already met some of them in this book!) Others need a little more time. Mary Harris was one of those people. Her life was filled with tragedy and hardship from the time she was a little girl. There was no time to daydream when she was growing up, just hard work and struggle. She thought of nothing but survival until she was in her 30s, and even then, she was mostly just getting by. It took her entire life falling apart for her to find her true calling. After she picked up the pieces and built something new, it took some time for the rest of the world to catch up. Most of the country wouldn't even know her name until she was well over 60 years old. But by then, she was famous, a terror to the bosses and a comfort to the workers.

Mary Harris was born in the Irish city of Cork in 1837. Her family was Catholic, and nuns at a local convent taught

Mary how to read and write. There wasn't much time for her to get lost in her books, though; there were chores to do, prayers to say, and lessons to learn. It was a typical life for a poor man's daughter, but when she was seven, in the year 1845, something strange happened. Ireland's farmers started seeing mold growing all over their potatoes. Then the potatoes began to rot. The fields turned black with slime and decay, and the entire potato crop was destroyed.

This was an incredibly bad situation. Many other crops grew in Ireland's fertile soil, but the majority of its produce was exported over to England. All that was left was potatoes, which the population depended on as their main food source. At the time, Ireland was ruled by the English government, and the Irish were treated as second-class citizens in their own county. They had no control over their own economy, and the English enforced their laws at gunpoint. When the potato blight came, it wiped out most of the 1845 harvest—and with it, the most important food source for the entire population. With the potatoes gone, things started getting worse. Much worse.

Once the crops failed, there was hardly any other food left. What little was available became far too expensive for most people to afford. Landlords kicked people out of their homes when they ran out of money. Sick and starving people were everywhere. Over the next five years, over one million Irish people died from hunger, malnutrition, and disease. They called it the Great Hunger, and it was a time of unimaginable suffering. All the while, the English refused to send food over to Ireland to alleviate the famine. Mary and her family survived the first few years, but knew that they could not last much longer. Mary's family joined a mass exodus of Irish people who were forced to leave their homes in search of basic resources and the hope of a better life. Mary's father and brother sailed to the U.S. when Mary was 10 and settled in Toronto, Canada. Mary and her mother joined them three or four years later, crowding into one of the leaky old ships that ferried thousands of Irish immigrants across the sea.

Now that they had managed to find some stability, Mary began to plan her future. At that time, the Irish faced severe discrimination in the U.S. and were looked down upon for their culture and religion. As a woman, an immigrant, and an Irish person, there were very few career paths open to her. Her mother had already taught her how to sew and make clothes, so she had a leg up in that department. It would have been simple enough to become a dressmaker, but instead Mary decided she wanted to become a teacher. It was a respectable profession, and might allow her to see a bit of the world. It took some time, but when she was 23, she found a teaching job in Monroe, Michigan. She stayed there for about a year, but it wasn't the right fit. Maybe her mother had been right, because then Mary moved to

Chicago and found work as a dressmaker. The big, bustling city was a hotbed of industry, manufacturing, and labor organizing, but she still felt restless sitting at her sewing machine. When the urge to move hit her again, Mary moved South to Memphis, Tennessee. There was a large Irish population there, and Mary found another teaching job. She also met a man named George Jones.

He was a skilled ironworker and was a member of the International Iron Molders Union. He made decent wages and was respected by his fellow workers. For Mary, who had already endured more poverty and hardship than anyone ever should, this was more than enough to qualify him as a good partner. They got married in 1860. Their family grew quickly, and soon they had four children—three girls and a boy. Mary had her hands full taking care of them, but the future seemed bright. She'd built a home and family of her own. They had food in the pantry and clothes on their backs, clothes she'd probably sewn herself after her teaching day was over. It was enough, but it was not to last. In 1867, the year her youngest child and namesake, Mary, was born, tragedy struck again.

Memphis was a port city that never seemed to stop moving. Its arteries were clogged with steamboats and trains coming and going each day, and workers jumped on and off as it pleased them. It was an exciting place to live, but it attracted some extremely unwanted guests. Lots of those vehicles carried unseen passengers like insects and rodents, and they in turn carried diseases. Bacteria thrived in those conditions, and swampy Memphis was accustomed to dealing with outbreaks. In 1867, Memphis was hit by a massive yellow fever epidemic like nothing the city had ever seen before. Yellow fever is a nasty disease that causes vomiting, fever, liver failure, and ultimately death. People did not understand how it was contracted—they tended to blame diseases on bad smells and decaying matter—so there was nothing to stop the mosquitos from continuing its spread. It took over the entire area, and thousands of people lost their lives. Most of them were poor or working-class, like Mary and her family. Soon, Mary's husband and all four of their children became sick with yellow fever. She nursed them day and night, praying for them to recover, but there was no use. All five of them succumbed to the disease. At the age of 30, Mary was suddenly all alone.

Some people would have given up at that point, but Mary was a survivor. Death was nothing new, but it had taken far too much from her this time. She packed up her belongings and her sadness and moved back to Chicago. She was a widow with no family in the city, so there was no other option but for her to dive right back into work. She opened up a dressmaker's shop and buried her emotions. Life had already taught her that poor and working-class people didn't get time off to grieve. She eked out a living sewing dresses for wealthy upper-class women, working her fingers to the bone to sew their finery. As the candles burned low each night and she looked down at her cramped fingers, she thought a lot about the unfairness of their respective situations. She struggled for every crust of bread she ate, while the people who employed her dined on ice cream and champagne each night. "I would look out of the plate glass windows and see the poor, shivering wretches, jobless and hungry, walking alongside the frozen lake front," she once said. "My employers seemed neither to notice nor to care."

In 1871, just when Mary was starting to do well, another tragedy hit. The Great Chicago Fire consumed the city, killing 300 people in three days. Seventeen thousand buildings burned down. One of them was Mary's shop, which had all of her dressmaking materials and personal possessions inside. Once again, she was forced to start over. Her new shop just happened to be next door to the Knights of Labor's office, a working people's association that brought together workers from different industries and backgrounds to advocate for their rights. Their biggest goals were to implement a standard eight-hour workday and end child labor. This especially appealed to Mary, who never forgot her lost children. She began attending Knights of Labor meetings after work. Child labor was everywhere. Her neighborhood was full of scrawny, tired children who worked in Chicago's factories and slaughterhouses. She knew how dangerous the work was, and how badly it harmed their little bodies. Some of them were missing fingers or hands; others were stooped over like old people. Their adult coworkers weren't doing much better. It pained Mary to see how hard life still was for so many of her neighbors, and she thought again of her children.

Wanting to channel her energy and emotions into something productive, she became very involved in the Knights of Labor. She found her voice, and the once-quiet teacher began organizing strikes and protests. Mary became known as a powerful speaker with a talent for firing up crowds with her bombastic speeches. As time went on, she grew more and more confident. She began traveling the country talking to workers and encouraging them to join unions. Her reputation began to precede her, and strikers would request visits from her to their own picket lines. Mary was getting older, and always wore black as a sign of mourning for her family. With her glasses and cloud of white hair, others saw her as the grandmother of the labor movement. Her strong voice and soft heart made people trust her, while her passion and fearlessness made them respect her. Left without her own family, she adopted the workers of the world as her own. She called them her "boys." They called her Mother Jones.

And she had room in her heart for everyone. Unlike

many labor figures of her day, Jones did not discriminate against women or Black workers. She would later cofound the Industrial Workers of the World, a labor union that welcomed all workers into the fold regardless of race or gender. Alongside Lucy Parsons, she was the only woman invited to serve as a cofounder. She was particularly enthusiastic about encouraging women and families to get involved in strikes instead of staying back at home while the men picketed. Mary would organize wives into "mop and bucket" brigades to fight alongside their husbands on the picket lines and cheered as the women faced off against angry bosses and guards. Family was important to her, and she saw strong working-class families as the building blocks that would bring people up out of poverty. Mary also thought that women didn't get enough credit for their bravery and capability. She certainly wasn't going to stay home while the miners were fighting for what was right, so why should they?

When the Knights of Labor became inactive, Mary began working as an organizer for the United Mine Workers. The miners' union had a reputation for being tough. They had to be—the job was brutal, and coal mine owners hated unions. They had no interest in listening to the workers' demands or treating them like anything less than beasts of burden. It was a powerful industry that kept the nation's lights on, but the miners themselves could barely afford soap to wash the coal dust off their faces. In 1897, 9,000 coal miners in Pennsylvania went on strike and Mary showed up to help. Thanks to her years with the Knights, she had become an extremely effective organizer as well as a tremendous speaker. The union was so impressed they sent her down into the Appalachian coalfields to help them organize more miners. She encouraged the workers to come together to fight for their right to unionize and for better treatment. Doing so was risky, and they all knew the potential consequences. It was a violent time, when mine owners would send armed guards into the coalfields to bully and attack the pro-union miners. The miners refused to give up, even when things got bloody. Of course, Mary was in the middle of it all, and her commitment to their fight led to her being known as the "miners' angel."

Though the coal miners held on to a big piece of her heart, Mary did not forget about the children, either. They remained one of her main priorities, and she didn't let people forget about their plight. As she told a crowd of striking silk mill workers in 1900, "The American people were born in strikes, and now in the closing days of the 19th century, even the children must strike for justice." At the time, 18 percent of American workers were under the age of 16. It hurt Mary's heart to see them coming out of the mines covered in coal dust or walking into the factories with their mangled limbs and hollow eyes. She was disgusted to live in a country where wealthy industrialists got rich off the backs of children.

In 1903, she was still with the miners in West Virginia when she heard about a new strike happening up north. One hundred thousand workers in the Kensington district of Philadelphia, PA, had walked out of the drafty, dirty mills on July 1. Sixteen thousand of them were children as young as ten. Instead of going to school or playing outside, the mill children spent 12 hours a day packing clothes, sweeping floors, working machinery, and doing many other jobs in the area's huge garment factories. The workers had asked the factory owners to shorten their workweek by five hours, from 60 to 55. The extra few hours would have given them a little more time to learn, or sleep, or play. But the bosses refused. They told the workers that they were ungrateful. In response, the workers called for a strike.

When Mary heard about what was happening, she hurried up to Philadelphia. When she arrived, she demanded to know why the local newspapers weren't printing stories about the strike. The reporters told her that the mill owners were too powerful, and they were scared to lose their jobs. Annoyed at their cowardice, Mary called a mass meeting and invited reporters from New York City to do it instead. "Philadelphia's mansions [are] built on the broken bones, the quivering hearts, and drooping heads of these children," she told the crowd. The child workers stood on a platform alongside her and showed the press their missing limbs.

She didn't stop there. When she saw how much publicity the children had gotten in Philadelphia, she decided to take their crusade nationwide. After all, child labor was a problem everywhere, not just in one city. She'd seen that firsthand. So Mary met with the Textile Workers Union and hatched a plan. She would lead hundreds of child workers and their parents on a long march up the East Coast to New York City. From there they would pay a visit to President Theodore Roosevelt's New York summer home and ask him to meet with them. They would also make stops along the way to talk about the children's plight, shame business owners who hired children, and raise money for the strike. It became known as "The March of the Mill Children." The children who marched were called Mother Jones's Army.

After Mary got their parents' permission, about 100 children joined her and several grown-up members of the Textile Workers Union. They walked and walked and walked some more. It was 125 miles from Philadelphia to New York City, and their little legs could only go so far in a day. Along the way, they visited former president Grover Cleveland's mansion in Princeton, New Jersey, but his staff shooed them away and would not allow them to camp on his property for the night. The children didn't mind, though; all the time outdoors was a novelty for them, and they appreciated having a break from work. They stopped to rest when they could, and breathed in as much of the fresh air as they could. The march wasn't easy, but it was a lot better than a loud, dusty factory. And Mary was a kind, motherly leader. She cared deeply about the children and believed in their cause. When their shoes wore out, Mary bought them new ones; when their clothes tore, she mended them. She made sure that they had time to play, too, and to act like the kids they still were. That march was the first vacation they'd ever had.

When they reached New York City, the children paraded through the streets while Mary spoke about the strike. It had been a long three weeks, and she knew that they all needed a break. The march had gotten a good deal of attention, but the politicians hadn't made any actual promises yet. There was still a lot of work to do, but it was time to rest—and play. Mary came up with a special treat for her army, most of whom had never seen the ocean before. The children spent two days in Coney Island enjoying the beach and the amusement park. They needed more than a vacation; they needed a chance to have fun, to run and jump and act like children. Their lives had been shaped by hard work and empty bellies. The march would not last forever, and soon enough the children would have to go back to work. For those two days at least, Mary wanted them to feel special.

President Roosevelt had plenty of advance notice that they were coming. Mary had sent him two letters asking for a meeting and told reporters they were on their way. When it came time to visit the president, though, the doors stayed closed. He refused to meet with Mary or any of the children because he wanted to enjoy his *own* vacation. Staring down at their hopeful little faces would have ruined his good mood and reminded him of how badly he had failed them. Mary had been prepared for the worst, but it still came as a slap in the face to the children who had come so far. They had hoped that the famously rough-and-tumble president would listen to them and use his power to help. Instead, they had to travel back to Philadelphia empty-handed. Mary was spitting mad about it, too; she told reporters that "Teddy was scared of me" and never forgave him for letting her army down. But despite how awful they felt that day, their efforts were not in vain. A few years later, the state of Pennsylvania passed stronger child labor laws. It raised the legal working age to 14 and set a maximum workweek of 58 hours. Progress came slowly, but it came.

President Roosevelt had had good reason to be scared of Mary. She was known as "the most dangerous woman in America" for her ironclad commitment to workers' rights and absolute fearlessness in the face of danger. She faced down armed guards and death threats, was thrown in jail multiple times, and was tailed by police wherever she popped up. In 1914, when miners were on strike in Ludlow, Colorado, the police locked her up before she even got a chance to speak to the workers—they thought she would cause too much trouble. On April 20, the Colorado National Guard soldiers joined private armed guards employed by the Colorado Fuel and Iron Company to attack a strike camp in Ludlow. They murdered 21 people, most of them women and children. News of the Ludlow Massacre horrified the nation, and Mary made sure that their story was not forgotten. "Pray for the dead and fight like hell for the living!" she would say. She even testified about it in front of Congress.

As the years went on, it got harder for Mary to keep up her punishing schedule. Sometimes she yearned to rest her weary bones, but she knew that the people needed her, so she continued to push onward. She continued to organize, agitate, and travel for the rest of her life, refusing to slow down until she was physically unable to keep going. "My address is like my shoes," she once said. "It travels with me. I abide where there is a fight against wrong." Mary continued to work with the United Mine Workers until the early 1920s. She made her last public strike appearance in 1924, when she showed up to a picket line to support striking dressmakers. As a former dressmaker herself, their struggle reminded her of her own, all those years ago.

In 1925, she decided to write her autobiography and share the story of her colorful life. Mary could no longer hold a pen between her fingers, though, so she asked a journalist named Mary Field Parton to help. Mary told the other Mary her life story as she recalled it, and the younger woman wrote it down. The book remains a classic of labor literature (even if some of the details are a little murky) and a wonderful read. Her health continued to decline, but Mary kept her sparkle. When she turned 92, workers, union leaders, politicians, and friends all gathered to throw her a big party—and to say goodbye.

The fiery Irishwoman who was once referred to by the United States Senate as the "grandmother of all agitators" got her wish in the end. She had once said, "I hope to live long enough to be the great-grandmother of all agitators." After six decades of raising hell, Mary "Mother Jones" Harris died at the age of 93 on November 30, 1930. She is buried in the Union Miners Cemetery in Mount Olive, Illinois, next to some of her beloved coal miners. Even in death, she refused to abandon her "boys"—the workers who gave her purpose, fought by her side, and ultimately became her family. Now she'll never be alone again.

Eugene V. Debs
The Tireless Visionary
1855-1926

While there is a lower class, I am in it, while there is a criminal element, I am of it, and while there is a soul in prison, I am not free.

Eugene was never very interested in school. He preferred to look out the windows and daydream, counting down the minutes until he could escape the schoolhouse. Reading, writing, and arithmetic bored him, and sitting still was a torment. Though he was blessed with an incredible memory, he was more interested in the people around him over anything his teachers had to say. Eugene much preferred listening to his father, Daniel, talk about French and German philosophy, or read passages from their favorite author, Victor Hugo. Hugo's complex stories of love, war, poverty, and tumult were far more exciting than listening to his teacher drone on and on about letters and numbers.

Besides, there was a much wider world outside of school, and Eugene had already caught a glimpse of it. He was born in 1855 and was only five years old when the country went to war against itself. In 1869, the Civil

War had only recently ended, and his neighbors were still struggling to recover from the war's economic impacts. They needed a little extra help now and then, and Eugene was happy to give it. He might not have been a great student, but he had a big heart and a strong back. Helping out his neighbors when they needed it became his biggest hobby, and he became well-known around his hometown of Terre Haute, Indiana, for his good deeds. While his father expected him to spend most of his days working at the grocery store, Eugene somehow always had time to carry in a neighbor's groceries, or to help some local children fly a kite. As much as his father's customers appreciated him when Eugene was there, the store was an afterthought for him. He wanted more.

Coincidentally, 1869 also marked the year that the trains came to Terre Haute. Four new railroads had laid down tracks in town, connecting the city to the rest of the Midwest, the East Coast, and California. More people moved to Terre Haute itself, too, and its population exploded. All of a sudden, Eugene's sleepy little hometown had become a bustling center for trade, industry, and travel. It was thrilling to see. He had often looked out the windows of the grocery store and watched the railroad men working on the massive trains, imagining all the places they would get to see. By the time Eugene was 14, he had made up his mind. He would go out and find a new job—one that was exciting, and interesting, and got him out from behind that boring old counter. He wanted to work on the railroad.

It's hard to believe the idea of a 14-year-old boy working in such dangerous and physically demanding conditions, but in 1870, child labor was a common sight in his hometown, just like it was for Mary Harris in Philadelphia, Frances Perkins in New York, and Lucy Parsons in Chicago, among many others in this book. Terre Haute was in the middle of a labor shortage, and at six feet tall, Eugene looked like he could handle it. His parents were upset when he quit high school to concentrate on work, but they needed the money he could bring in. His first job on the rails was cleaning grease off the freight engines. It was cold, dirty, difficult work, and he was paid 50 cents a day to do it. The excitement he'd felt looking out the windows at the men who became his coworkers faded, but in its place, Eugene felt a great deal of pride about the hard work he was putting in—and the paycheck he was contributing to the family's finances. He'd found a new way to help the people he cared about, and it made his heart swell with happiness.

He was soon promoted to painter, and in 1871, he was brought on board the train itself to work as a fireman. In this context, a fireman's job was to help the engineer control the train by adding fuel to the locomotive's boiler. This was called "firing" the "firebox." Eugene was now making more than a dollar a day, which felt like a fortune to him. To his family's surprise, he used the extra money to give school another shot. Eugene began attending classes at a local business college, hoping to learn more about literature and railroad technology. This was on top of his job at the railroad, which was tough enough for someone so young. It was a brutal schedule to keep, and he didn't sleep much. When Eugene got laid off in 1873, his family hoped he would come back home. Instead, he found another railroad job in faraway St. Louis, which was an even bigger business city than his hometown.

It was a rude awakening for the gentle farm boy. The time he spent in St. Louis opened his eyes wide to the kind of poverty and misery that defined the lives of all too many poor and working people in America. He saw starving children playing in the mud, their families struggling to survive. It was a far cry from his own comfortable upbringing back in Terre Haute and it pained him to see people suffering. It made him appreciate the little things, which weren't all that little. His own job was no walk in the park, but he had a warm bed and food to eat. The railroad felt like a good place for him to be, and he didn't have any plans to give it up. In 1874, though, his mother wrote to him and begged him to come home. She missed him, of course, but she was mostly worried about him.

The rail companies often cut corners on safety and maintenance measures, and all the news of accidents, injuries, and deaths had terrified Eugene's mother. She couldn't stand it any longer, so she called Eugene home. It felt like a step back for him at the time. He was 19 years old, with little formal education and no idea what he wanted to do with his life. But the lessons he learned during his time on the railroad would stick with him. His experience as a fireman would define what he did next—and who he would become.

Once Eugene got back to Terre Haute, he took a job as a billing clerk at a large Midwestern grocery company. He wasn't very happy about being stuck behind a counter again, but did his best to make the days go by quickly. Just like during his school days, he'd watch the clock, waiting for what felt like his real life to begin. After his shift, he would walk down to the railroad tracks and catch up with his old friends. It was there that he heard the news that a leader from the Brotherhood of Locomotive Firemen (BLF) was coming to town. Eugene didn't know much about unions at that point, but was curious. He tagged along to the union meeting, liked what he heard, and ended up joining. That curiosity blossomed into a deep devotion to the cause of labor. The work of a union leader suited him, too. He spent hours and hours talking to railroad workers and finding out what kind of problems they faced. He had only spent a few years on the rails himself, but through the union, he met old-timers who had spent their entire lives working a dangerous job. They noticed how interested he was in solving their problems, so Eugene was soon elected secretary of his locality. The BLF was not a particularly active or militant union, but it was a good place to learn about the way the union worked and how it related to other parts of the labor movement.

In 1877, thousands of railroad workers in Pennsylvania, Maryland, and West Virginia went on strike. It was a long way away from Indiana, and Eugene's union was not involved, but he still watched the strike closely. It was his first real look at the dangerous side of becoming involved in the labor movement. What he saw filled him with horror. The president sent in federal troops to control the strikers. In Pittsburgh, the troops killed 26 people. The strike lasted 52 days and was the first strike in U.S. history to spread to multiple states. It was a formative moment for many who watched, including Eugene, and he became even more active in his own union after that.

Eugene might not have gotten much out of his formal education, but he was still a voracious reader. As Victor Hugo once wrote, "To learn to read is to light a fire," and his words inspired Eugene to push himself harder. The literary classics he loved so much also helped him train himself to become a masterful public speaker. The union noticed his way with words and in 1878, they gave him an editorial role at the union's monthly publication, *Locomotive Firemen's Magazine*. Two years later, he was promoted to editor and appointed grand secretary and treasurer of the BLF.

By and large, the railroad unions were more conservative than many of the other unions who were active during that era. They tried to avoid striking whenever possible, preferring to compromise or stay out of labor disputes altogether (which was one of the many reasons the 1877 strike was such a big deal!). The BLF promoted the idea that the rail bosses and the rail workers were "friends," a stance the railroad executives were eager to take advantage of for their own benefit. Early on, Eugene agreed with this more neutral viewpoint, but his perspective changed as he spent time in the labor movement and saw what strikes could accomplish.

His politics evolved, too, and he decided to run for local office to continue his mission of improving things for working people. He began his political career as a Democrat, serving two terms as Terre Haute's city clerk before he was elected to Indiana's General Assembly in 1884. Making it into the halls of power was a big accomplishment, but his time there didn't go well. He stuck out in more ways than one, and Eugene found it difficult to relate to his new coworkers. He tried his hardest to push through laws that would benefit workers, women, and Black Americans, but he continually saw his progressive agenda shot down. By the time his term was up, he was disgusted with the whole process. Worse, Eugene felt like he had failed his community. The thought chilled him to the bone, and he resolved to never run for political office again.

Instead, Eugene focused on the union. There were some big changes in his personal life, too: he fell in love. In 1885, he married a woman named Kate Metzel. She was as practical and polished as he was friendly and impulsive, and while he was off daydreaming, she focused more on day-to-day issues. Throughout their long lives together, Kate also ensured that Eugene looked after himself. His health was a constant concern, and she nursed him during his frequent bouts of illness. Without Kate's reminders, he would forget to rest, to eat, to do anything but work. She was his biggest supporter as well as his protector. If Eugene was feeling ill or tired and visitors appeared, they had to go through Kate first.

Much of their marriage was spent apart because Eugene was always on the road doing union business or political work. Meanwhile, Kate kept busy at home. She had her own well-developed political perspectives, too. She agreed with Eugene on many things and was especially passionate about women's suffrage. "The cause of woman's rights is advancing with the cause of man's intelligence," she once wrote. "And no matter how many obstacles may be thrown in its way by ignorance, prejudice and sordid self-interest, the time is coming when women will be the equal of man, when both will be free, when society will rise to a higher plane, and enter into a larger and nobler life."

They were a good match.

While Eugene's home life was settled, his relationship with the Brotherhood of Locomotive Firemen was growing more complicated. His evolving opinions about strikes and the conflicts between labor and capital did not fit into the other leaders' visions. Once again, he felt like the odd man out. In 1893, he decided to step down from his post as grand secretary of the union. He felt it was time to create a new kind of labor union, one that incorporated the more progressive political outlook he had slowly been developing. Eugene had become disillusioned with the craft model of unionism that the railroads practiced, in which workers were separated by craft. Each job had its own union, and those unions didn't always see eye to eye. In Eugene's opinion, it complicated things and kept workers from forming connections with one another. He wanted to try something new—and he did. After he left the BLF, Eugene founded the American Railway Union (ARU). It was the first industrial railroad union. That meant that under the ARU, all rail workers were welcome to join, with the idea that they would be in a better position to bargain stronger contracts and make demands. Instead of dividing workers into smaller groups, the ARU would build a strong, united membership.

The experiment was an immediate success. Within its first year, the ATU had gained thousands of members in 125 locations. Even better, the union's first strike, which took place against the Great Northern Railway, resulted in a win!

Eugene was thrilled. His vision of uniting the rail workers was coming to life. It had come together just in time, too, because in 1894, workers at the Pullman Palace Car rail company launched a huge strike that spread throughout the nation. That strike became the union's first large-scale battle, and it soon became clear that it would not be a fair fight. After the ARU declared a boycott of all Pullman cars, asking customers not to travel on them and to support the strike instead, the rail bosses and government both became very, very nervous. The last thing they wanted was to see the railroad's profits go down.

The union had hit them where it hurt—their pockets. The rail barons got together in their smoky offices and chewed cigars and argued with one another until a consensus was reached: the strike simply could not be allowed to continue. They had to use their considerable resources to crush this worker uprising, fast. Their first move was to bring in strikebreakers, who were hired to work in the union workers' place. That made the strikers anxious; would they have jobs to go back to after the strike was over? That uncertainty was exactly what the bosses wanted. Then, they used their political connections to convince the federal government to intervene in the strike. The federal government slapped Eugene and the ARU with an injunction (an order from a judge requiring a person to do or stop doing something) that forbade them from communicating with the striking union members. Then, the president sent troops into Chicago and other big rail hubs to break up the strike and prevent the workers from picketing. Just like in 1877, their presence resulted in more violence against the workers. The union workers did their best to hold on, but the strike and the ARU were both broken in the end. Eugene himself was arrested for violating the injunction—because of course he wasn't going to abandon his members—and was sentenced to six months in prison.

During his time behind bars, Eugene had many hours to think, read, and talk with the other residents of the Woodstock, Illinois prison. The political views he had been refining throughout his life finally crystallized and he began identifying as a socialist: someone who believes that workers should share ownership of the tools, land,

and buildings that they use to make products or provide services. The capitalist system in which only a handful of wealthy people own everything and keep the vast majority of the profits did not make sense to him. He thought back to the poverty-stricken families he'd seen in St. Louis as a teenager, and to the words of Victor Hugo: "Those who do not weep, do not see." Eugene had already seen too much suffering. He decided that socialism was the best way to end the exploitation, poverty, and hunger that afflicted so many poor and working people. Armed with this realization, Eugene would spend the rest of his life spreading the word of socialism wherever he went. He was not alone, either; many workers and members of the labor movement were socialists (and still are!). It was a time of great inequality, and those who had little were very much aware of how unfair it was that so few had so much. Socialism offered them an answer. "The red flag is the only race flag; it is the flag of revolt against robbery; the flag of the working class, the flag of hope and high resolve—the flag of Universal Freedom," Eugene once wrote about the famous socialist symbol.

Despite Eugene's earlier insistence that he did not want anything more to do with politics, he ended up spending the rest of his life involved in various political parties and causes. He was stubborn, but could never refuse a request from someone who needed him—and it turned out that a whole lot of people needed him to share his message widely. In 1898, he helped found the Social Democratic Party of America, and two years later, ran for president as a socialist. He got 96,116 votes that year, which wasn't too shabby for a brand-new left-wing political party! The Socialist Party nominated him for president five times in total, in 1900, 1904, 1908, 1912, and 1920. For good measure, he also ran for Congress at home in Terre Haute in 1916 (he lost that one, too—Eugene was many things, but he wasn't much of a politician).

Though he never again held political office, Eugene saw his multiple campaigns as an effective way to spread the message of socialism to workers across the country. His skills as a public speaker were legendary, and his reputation as a fighter for working people everywhere endeared him to the American public. When he showed up to speak, crowds gathered; when he rode the rails on his way to other destinations, railroad workers would thank him for what he'd done on their behalf. People could tell that he truly cared about them. It made them want him to win.

He may have been pulled back into politics, but the labor movement was where Eugene saw the most promise. Like many other socialists, he felt that organizing workers was far more important than winning votes or lobbying. In 1905, he joined with a group of other labor organizers to form another big industrial union—this time, one that was meant for all workers, not just the railroaders. It was called the Industrial Workers of the World (IWW). "The working class and the employing class have nothing in common," its constitution read. "There can be no peace so long as hunger and want are found among millions of the working people and the few, who make up the employing class, have all the good things of life." This made sense to Eugene, too. When Victor Hugo wrote, "The paradise of the rich is made out of the hell of the poor," he might as well have been speaking directly to Eugene and the other IWW founders.

Eugene made many friends throughout his career in labor, but not everyone appreciated his words or actions. Socialism was a controversial idea, and to many people, he was its most visible advocate. The U.S. government was well aware of his reputation as a troublemaker, and eventually caused a whole lot of trouble for him. As we read in Ben Fletcher's story, during World War I, the U.S. government enacted a series of severe restrictions on free speech in order to silence dissent and solidify support for the war. After the Espionage Act of 1917 and the Sedition Act of 1918 were passed, it became illegal to criticize the government. This presented a problem for Eugene, who opposed the war and had also spent years traveling the country loudly criticizing the government, politicians, and capitalism. Dissent was kind of his whole deal! But the timing was not in his favor. After those laws came into effect, many socialist newspapers and magazines were shut down (including several that Eugene wrote for). Anti-war voices were effectively silenced, and those who refused to comply risked severe punishments. The risk was there, but still, plenty of socialists and labor leaders like Eugene protested the crackdown on free speech. It horrified them to see their own government restricting citizens' ability to express their opinions on a controversial war. It wasn't fair, and more than that, it wasn't right. Some of them decided to take their chances and speak out anyway. Can you guess what Eugene did?

Of course he refused to be silent. Doing so would have gone against everything he stood for, and he wasn't afraid to go back to prison. His first stint behind bars had damaged his health, but it hadn't affected his spirit. So, in 1918, he went to a rally in Canton, Ohio, and delivered a long, passionate speech criticizing the government, the capitalists, and—briefly—the war. "The master class has always declared the wars; the subject class has always fought the battles," he roared, sweat dripping off his brow as he flung his arms out over the crowd. "The master class has had all to gain and nothing to lose, while the subject class has had nothing to gain and all to lose—especially their lives."

Government agents had been waiting for him in the

crowd. As he spoke, they hurriedly wrote down every word of his speech, making sure they caught the objectionable parts. When he finished speaking and stepped down off the stage, they moved in. Eugene was arrested for violating the Sedition Act and taken to jail. When it came time for him to stand trial, he asked to speak for himself instead of hiring a lawyer. The idea that he would receive a fair trial seemed laughable, so he thought he might as well use the opportunity to spread his message. He did the same at his sentencing hearing. There, he delivered one of the greatest speeches of his life. It was then that he uttered the immortal words, "Your Honor, years ago I recognized my kinship with all living beings, and I made up my mind that I was not one bit better than the meanest on earth. I said then, and I say now, that while there is a lower class, I am in it, and while there is a criminal element, I am of it, and while there is a soul in prison, I am not free."

Those words have since become a treasured part of American history and continue to inspire activists and labor leaders today. But at the time, the judge and jury were not impressed with his eloquence or his principles. They declared him guilty. Eugene didn't accept the verdict without a fight, but after taking his case all the way to the Supreme Court, Eugene was finally sentenced to 10 years in prison. At the time, he was 64 years old. He entered the Moundsville, West Virginia, prison on April 12, 1919, transferred to the

Atlanta Federal Penitentiary two months later, then settled in for the long haul. He kept busy inside by making friends with his fellow prisoners and guards alike, writing letters to his family and friends in the movement, and, of course, reading.

The next year, he made history by becoming the first person to ever run for president from inside a prison cell. That political bug just kept on biting him. That turned out to be the second most successful campaign he'd ever run, too. People didn't care that he was in prison; they still thought he was their best hope. Eugene won nearly one million votes, but Republican Warren G. Harding secured the election. After WWI ended in 1918, the public began to wonder if it was really necessary to keep all those antiwar protestors behind bars. The president began quietly releasing some of the people (like Ben Fletcher) who had been tossed into prison at the height of war fever. After receiving an avalanche of appeals on Eugene's behalf, President Harding finally commuted his sentence, too. Eugene was released from prison in 1921.

Eugene was happy to be home with Kate and his friends, but his years away had taken their toll. The constant travel and lack of rest had already started to wear him down even before his last arrest. He was 66 years old when he was finally released, and this second round of prison time had been rough on his already fragile health. Kate did everything she could to help him heal, but he never fully recovered. "I am not ill, but for the first time in my life I feel tired and worn," he always insisted. He fought it until the end, but on October 20, 1926, his big, brave heart—the heart that had driven him to dedicate his life to workers and endeared him to millions—finally failed him. Eugene Victor Debs died at the age of 70, having followed his own advice until the end: "Be true to yourself and you cannot be a traitor to any good cause on earth."

Rosina Tucker
The Brotherhood's Keeper
1881–1987

While I live, let not my life be in vain. And when I depart, may there be remembrance of me and my life as I have lived it.

Rosina was nervous. It was a hot day, and her hands felt sticky with sweat as she held tight to an envelope. She tried to look cool and calm as she walked along the train platform. The noise of clattering trains and shouting railroad workers filled the air around her, but she did her best to block it out. This wasn't her first time delivering this kind of envelope; she'd done it many times before, yet it always felt like walking into the lion's den. She knew if the company's men saw what she was carrying, she would be in serious trouble. People were depending on her, though, so Rosina kept moving. There was no time to be afraid. She had a train to catch.

Rosina, whose full name was Rosina Budd Harvey Corrothers Tucker, was traveling from New York City to Washington, D.C., to deliver a message for her friend, A. Philip Randolph. He was the president of a new union called the Brotherhood of Sleeping Car Porters, and Rosina was helping him with organizing. It was her job to securely deliver messages between him and Ashley Totten, a railroad porter who helped found the union. Their messages had to stay secret, because if railroad management caught them communicating, they would punish the union's members. It was a tense time on the rails. The workers couldn't afford to lose their jobs, but there were not yet any federal laws that guaranteed their right to unionize. In order to conduct union business, they had to go underground. The bosses were angry that the workers were organizing and wanted to stop their union campaign from succeeding. Unfortunately for them, Rosina was a very good organizer—and she was fearless.

She was born on November 4, 1881. Her parents had been born into slavery in Virginia and moved to Washington, D.C., after Emancipation. Education was important to their family, and her father made sure that she and her siblings had good foundational knowledge in many subjects, including in music. Rosina loved playing the piano and was a talented student. When she was 17 years old, she married a man named James Corrothers and moved around for a few years while they tried to find their footing. They eventually moved back to Rosina's hometown of Washington, D.C., where she would stay for the rest of her life. She was a religious woman, and the church was a huge part of their daily lives. James was a minister and a poet, and Rosina worked as a music teacher and a church organist.

When James died unexpectedly in 1917, Rosina's world turned upside down. She had gone directly from her parents' house to her marriage with James, and she wasn't used to being on her own. It was a little daunting to have to fend for herself, but Rosina found a way to make it work. She got a new job as a file clerk for the U.S. government. Love might have been the last thing on her mind at that busy point in her life, but it managed to find her anyway. Later that year she met a man named Berthea J. Tucker, and soon knew she would no longer be alone. He had a steady job working as a porter taking care of passengers on railroad tycoon George Pullman's sleeping cars, the fancy railroad cars that were used for long journeys by those who could afford them. They were married in 1918.

Berthea (known as B.J.) made more than Rosina did in her clerk position, but his job was much more physically demanding. As a rule, Pullman porters were expected to work very long hours for low pay. They were in constant motion, and seldom found time to rest on overnight trips. Porters were responsible for ensuring safety on the train and also had to know how the mechanical features of the cars worked. They were expected to attend to passengers' every request with a smile, no matter how rude or inappropriate, and strained their backs opening and putting away the heavy berth beds over and over again. The color line was strictly enforced; Pullman only hired Black men as porters, and white men as conductors. Pullman assumed that Black workers would be easier to control since they had fewer employment prospects, and took advantage of their need for steady work to pay them low wages.

Because their paychecks were so thin, porters depended on tips to help make ends meet. They could not risk upsetting their customers, so they had to put up with all kinds of disrespect and abuse during their workdays. The modern tipping system that still dominates the service industry today actually first started on Pullman cars. George Pullman implemented tipping so he could pay the porters less, while also making sure that they would act the way he wanted. He boasted of how "well-behaved" his Pullman workers were. Any porter who failed at being "diligent and cheerful" enough risked losing his job. In 1926, Rosina's husband would have made about $72.50 per month, plus whatever tips he received.

Despite all the downsides, Pullman porter jobs were highly sought after by many men. Porters were well-respected in their communities because it was the most prestigious job available to Black men during that period. Porters would even pass down their positions to their sons. But by 1925, the porters were sick and tired of being treated as less-than, tired of their low wages, and tired of being pushed around. Their jobs might have won them respect at home, but respect didn't keep the lights on or ease their aches and pains. A group of them got together and decided to do something about it.

What they did was start a union. The International Brotherhood of Sleeping Car Porters and Maids was formed by three Pullman porters, Ashley Totten, Roy Lancaster, and William H. Des Versey, with assistance from labor organizers Milton P. Webster and Asa Philip Randolph. Randolph was a busy and ambitious man. He had experience organizing dockworkers with the National Brotherhood of Workers of America, an early federation of Black unions. He was also the publisher of *The Messenger*, the country's most prominent radical Black newspaper. The porters had reached out to him to help them organize their union because of his experience in labor and his skills as a public speaker. As a bonus, since he did not work for Pullman, the company was unable to retaliate against him. He was as close as they could get to an insurance policy.

Unfortunately, Pullman was totally free to punish the porters themselves if and when the bosses caught wind of what they were planning. When the union went public, Pullman began firing organizers and pro-union workers in an effort to break up the Brotherhood before it got off the ground. Company spies monitored the porters, looking for pro-union sentiments. In an effort to intimidate the Black workforce, Pullman hired a large number of Filipino porters for the first time. His intention was to show the union that he considered their members to be disposable. Things had gotten ugly, and it was still early in the union campaign. It was an intensely stressful time for the porters, and they needed as much help as they could get. That's where Rosina came in.

Rosina had first met A. Philip Randolph in Washington, D.C., in the early 1920s. They stayed in touch, and she hosted early Brotherhood meetings in her home. Six weeks after the union was founded, she and other porters' wives, family members, and Pullman maids came together to form the Colored Women's Economic Council. (This group would later become known as the Ladies Auxiliary and would have chapters wherever the union had a presence.) Rosina became the council's first president. She also became an organizer for the Brotherhood itself. The company's firm opposition to the union meant that she had to be careful. They couldn't punish her directly, but her husband still worked for Pullman. She had to protect him and the other workers as well as herself. "We would have to act in secret because if the management found out, they would fire people," she once said. "That's why, in one sense, it was easier for the wives to do the work. That's how I got involved."

Rosina was a one-woman organizing force. In addition to delivering important messages, she would also go door-to-door at Pullman porters' homes to convince them to join the union. When she was successful, she would then get their wives to join the Economic Council. As far as Rosina was concerned, the union's goal of improving working conditions and raising wages for porters would help the whole family, and she stressed that message when she spoke with reluctant Pullman workers. She was as careful as she could be, but the company's spies were everywhere. In 1928, her worst nightmare came to life when her husband, Berthea, was fired over his involvement in the union. His bosses had learned about Rosina's organizing work and were furious that this woman has caused them so much grief. They wanted them both gone. But when she found out about her husband's firing, Rosina marched right into the Pullman office and demanded that they give him his job back. Her bold action worked, and he was back on the train the next day. Rosina had made it clear that she was not about to let some company stooge boss her around.

Besides sticking up for her husband and his male coworkers, she also wanted to help the Black women who worked alongside the porters as maids. Pullman maids shared many of the same challenges that the porters faced but had to navigate an extra layer of sexism. Their duties were to clean the cars and provide intimate services to female passengers, like hairdressing, mending clothes, and giving free manicures. Like the porters, maids were also expected to take care of passengers' children, elders, and sick people on their routes. They had to buy their own supplies, from sewing needles to nail files. They were often the only female crew members in their car and were not allowed to socialize with the passengers or their male coworkers. It was a lonely job, especially for those who were mothers and had children of their own waiting back home. Their wages were higher than what Black women in other domestic service jobs could expect, but even after the union became established, maids were still paid less than porters. The position was only open to Black female applicants until 1925, when the company began hiring Chinese women to work its Western routes.

The double bind of sexism and racism they faced as Black women workers set the Pullman maids apart from their railroad brothers. The Brotherhood did not allow the Pullman maids to join, so they had to join the auxiliary Rosina set up instead. Their relationship with the other women in the auxiliary was complicated, too. Many of the wives (of the union men) believed that the union's job was to raise the men's wages high enough that the women would be able to stay home as respectable housewives. They wanted to entirely avoid the dirty, low-paid domestic service jobs that were the only paid work available to Black women. The white wives of union men got to stay home and rely on their husbands' wages; why shouldn't they be able to do the same?

Rosina did not agree with this view. She understood how the other wives felt, but wanted to unionize women workers, too. It was important to her to encourage women's independence. By growing the labor movement, she thought that workers would be able to demand better for themselves and the next generation. She wanted the Brotherhood's auxiliary to become "the big sisters" of the labor unions that were to come. "My heart is in the labor movement," she said at the auxiliary's 1938 convention. A smaller group of auxiliary members joined her in trying to uplift Black women workers alongside their brothers. It was a noble but challenging goal. At that point, even the union itself wasn't treating the Pullman maids fairly—the women were treated like second-class members of their own union. And not only did the Brotherhood keep them from officially joining, it also left them out of its first big victory.

After becoming the first Black-led union to be admitted into the American Federation of Labor in 1935, the Brotherhood made history again in 1937. That year, the union finally finished its negotiations with the Pullman Company. The result was the first-ever union contract between a Black labor union and a major American corporation. The contract included raises for both porters and maids, but the union leaders had agreed to a version of the contract that allowed the maids to still be paid less than the porters. The women also lost their seniority rights, which had guaranteed that maids who had been working there the longest got their first choice of travel routes. This made a big difference, especially for maids who had families; being sent to faraway California instead of New York, for example, meant that a maid would have much less time to rest and go home. It was something that impacted their lives outside of work as well as their time on the job, but the union's male leadership didn't see it that way. In order to reach a deal, they agreed to the company's demand to get rid of the seniority system. It doesn't seem like much of a coincidence that later that same year, the union officially dropped the "Maids" from its original name.

Meanwhile, auxiliary members like Rosina and her friends kept doing everything they could to drum up support for the Brotherhood. They used their experience fundraising for churches and civic organizations to raise money for the Brotherhood. A number of high-profile radical and progressive women like Floria Pinkney, the first Black organizer for the International Ladies' Garment Workers' Union, Lillian Herstein of the Chicago American Teachers' Union, Rose Schneiderman of the Women's

Trade Union League, the IWW's Elizabeth Gurley Flynn, and investigative journalist Ida B. Wells all donated resources to the Brotherhood. One slightly awkward fact about the movement—at least to the men who looked to pretend they were in charge of everything—was that it was not only women's labor that kept the union afloat, it was also their money. Randolph's wife, Lucille, used her social connections to help bankroll the Brotherhood's early years. (She also financially supported Randolph until he began drawing a salary in 1936.)

Even though they did not always get the respect they deserved, Rosina and the other auxiliary women never stopped fighting for the union. "If we never have another bite to eat, we will still fight for the Brotherhood," auxiliary member Lucy Bledsoe Gilmore once told a crowd in St. Louis. "I am like a rubber ball; the harder you throw me, the higher I bounce."

The vital organizing and political work that these women did for so many years also helped clear a path for the next generation. Later, Rosina became involved in the civil rights movement alongside her friend A. Philip Randolph. Though they had had their disagreements, he deeply respected all of her work for the union and her commitment to improving the lives of Black workers. In 1941, he announced that the Brotherhood was going to sponsor a huge march on Washington calling for full citizenship rights for Black people, an end to racial discrimination in the military and in unions, and Black self-government in colonized Africa and the Caribbean. He asked Rosina to help, knowing that she could be counted on to organize workers (and if necessary, keep strategy secrets). When President Franklin Delano Roosevelt found out about their plan, though, he reached out to Randolph and asked him to cancel the march. The president wanted to avoid raising any tensions with all their talk of equality and racial discrimination. In exchange, President Roosevelt signed Executive Order 8802, which banned discriminatory employment practices by federal agencies and in unions and created a Fair Employment Practices Committee to enforce it.

Twenty years later, A. Philip Randolph revisited the idea for a big march, and this time, nobody got in their way. He and labor organizer Bayard Rustin would organize the 1963 March on Washington for Jobs and Freedom to demand full civil and economic rights for Black Americans. It was one of the largest protests in American history and led to the passage of the Civil Rights Act of 1964. Once again, Rosina was one of the first people they called to help them plan the march. She was 82 years old and had spent her entire life fighting for justice. They knew they could count on her.

Rosina Tucker never stopped fighting, either. She continued her organizing work in Washington, D.C., for decades. True to her long-held belief that all women workers need unions, she used her organizing experience to help domestic workers and laundry workers. She also stayed very active in local politics and civic organizations, and was especially interested in public education. As the years went by, people began to recognize Rosina and her co-organizers for the historic figures they were. In 1982, she was asked to narrate a documentary about the Brotherhood of Sleeping Car Porters and its auxiliary called *Miles of Smiles, Years of Struggles*. She also wrote an autobiography called *My Life As I Have Lived It*, which tells the story of an incredible life and an endless dedication to workers' rights.

As her old friend Randolph said, she had "an impressive personality and a brilliant mind." She never stopped using either and was a union woman until the very end. Rosina died on March 3, 1987, at the age of 105.

Maria Moreno
The Mother of a Movement
1920-1989

I'm an American citizen, and I'm talking for justice.

It wasn't long after the flood had washed away her family's temporary home that Maria hit her breaking point. It was 1958, and two weeks of torrential rain had caused the rivers in Tulare County, California, to rise. Maria watched warily as the water crept higher and higher, praying that it would stop. Life was already hard enough for her and her family without adding bad weather to the equation. After 16 days, her fears came true when the swollen rivers finally flooded. Muddy water swept through the camp where she and hundreds of others lived. It destroyed their fragile shelters, washed away their belongings, and buried everything in mud. The disaster left 300 farmworkers—including Maria—homeless. As she sifted through the wreckage, wondering what would happen next, she quickly realized that the flood was only the beginning of their problems.

At the time, Tulare County and nearby Visalia were

both home to many migrant workers like her who had traveled there looking for jobs in the area's thriving agricultural industry. Years earlier, during the 1930s, hundreds of thousands of families had arrived in California after fleeing the Dust Bowl. A severe drought had stricken their farms on the prairies of Oklahoma, Kansas, Nebraska, and Texas, kicking up dust storms and killing crops. The Dust Bowl lasted from 1930 to 1936 and caused widespread poverty and starvation. Maria was only 10 years old when the crisis hit her home state of Texas. It would change the course of her life in many unexpected ways.

She had already dealt with so much. Born to a Mexican father and Mescalero Apache mother in 1920, Maria Torres Martinez began working in the fields alongside her parents when she was only eight years old. Farmworkers were paid very low wages, and just like in the cities, child labor was a common sight in the fields as well. Parents would bring their kids along with them to work and depended on their combined paychecks to support the family. In that way at least, not much had changed since the 1800s. It took an entire family's labor to keep a roof over their heads and their bellies full. The reason the wages were so low was because the government did not require the growers who owned the farmland to pay the workers a living wage. So, to maximize their own earnings, the growers chose to pay the workers barely anything at all. They didn't really care about how hard the farmworkers had to work as a result. It was tough for the workers to speak out against this inhumane treatment, too. They knew that they were at a severe disadvantage. The National Labor Relations Act (NLRA) of 1935 had protected many workers' right to unionize, but farmworkers were left out of the legislation. They had zero protections from bad bosses and no legal right to form a union.

Maria had to grow up fast. When she was 15 years old, she married 21-year-old Luis Moreno, a farmworker like herself. In 1940, the couple joined the Dust Bowl migration and moved to California in search of more fertile ground. They hoped that things would be easier—or at least, less dusty. The Morenos and thousands of other Latino migrant workers got jobs picking produce in the Golden State's huge fields and orchards. It was easy enough to find work; California's agricultural economy was huge, and there was a great need for people to pick and package its fruit and vegetables. The work was seasonal, though. Maria's family followed the harvest to survive, picking different kinds of produce all over the West Coast. There never seemed to be time to rest—there was always another harvest to tend to or bill to pay.

Maria and Luis had 12 children, four sons and eight daughters. As their family grew, so did their expenses. No matter how hard Maria, Luis, and their two adult sons worked, they still only brought home as little as $114 a week. With 14 people to feed, clothe, and shelter, the money never stretched far. Then, when the floods came in 1958, it wiped out what little stability they had been able to build. Their makeshift house was no match for the raging floodwaters. "Everything was gone," her eldest daughter Lilly DeLaTorre remembered. "My mom went to ask for help, and no one would help."

Their entire community of migrant workers was thrown into chaos. Finding food quickly became difficult, if not impossible. Farmworkers were not eligible for government food assistance, either, so they were left to figure it out on their own. Many of them began to starve. Maria's youngest child was still a baby when the flood came, and all she had to feed her was water and sugar. Meanwhile, the older children ate potato peel soup and boiled greens. Sometimes their parents ate nothing at all. Maria tried to hide the worst of it from her children. Survival was a daily battle, though, and the family's suffering was immense. Maria's big-hearted eldest son, 19-year-old Abel, was especially worried about his little brothers and sisters. He himself had begun working in the fields when he was five. Eventually, Abel stopped eating. Doing so meant that his younger siblings would have a little more food on their plates. But the strong young man's body needed nutrients too. It got harder and harder for him to get through the day. He ultimately had to be hospitalized for malnourishment. To his mother's horror, he also lost his sight for three days.

That was the last straw. Maria began speaking out publicly about her family's plight and how much the farmworkers' families were struggling. "I see the people that buy delicious apples, bananas, all kinds of good foods, and then I take a look at my table—beans and potatoes!" she cried in one speech. "How do you think that I feel, seeing my son blind because we don't got nothing to eat, while some other tables are full and wasting food!"

Maria's story was hard to ignore, and people began to take notice. *Fresno Bee* reporter Ron Taylor came to see her speak. Her words moved him. Ron wrote an article about Abel's blindness and the farmworkers' misery. Maria's words continued to spread after that. In 1959, she was asked to testify in front of the California Industrial Welfare Association. By sharing her family's story of suffering, she showed people that the farmworkers were not invisible—and that they desperately needed help. The additional public attention pushed the state welfare board to reverse its policy and extend food assistance to the farmworkers. Without Maria's bravery and Abel's sacrifice, the entire farmwork community would have been left to starve.

U.S.-born workers like Maria and her family were not

the only people working these back-breaking agricultural jobs or suffering under greedy employers. In 1942, the U.S. created the Bracero Program, an agreement with the Mexican governments that allowed Mexican workers to fill seasonal jobs on U.S. farms and railroads. This program expanded upon WWI-era efforts to effectively import Mexican workers to fill holes in the wartime labor market. Employers welcomed the influx of cheap, exploitable labor. However, labor organizations like the American Federation of Labor and Congress of Industrial Organizations (AFL-CIO) then led by President Samuel Gompers, resisted what they saw as competition for (white) American jobs. Gompers was concerned with his existing members. This closed-minded approach meant that the AFL-CIO missed out on a huge opportunity to organize farmworkers. Instead, the AFL-CIO abandoned them. It stopped working majority-Latino unions in the Southwest and refused to organize Latino workers for decades afterward. The Mexican workers themselves were met with racism, xenophobia, and violence. They were criticized and threatened for "taking American jobs." All the while, their employers were profiting off their lack of protections.

That early anti-Mexican prejudice led to a modern wave of repression. Between 1931 and 1933, President Herbert Hoover enacted a massive deportation raid on people of Mexican descent, in which up to 1.8 million Latinos—nearly 60 percent of whom were U.S. citizens—were forcibly removed to Mexico. In 1954, President Eisenhower did the same thing, deporting over 1 million more Latino people. As all this state-sponsored chaos played out, the AFL-CIO finally began to warm up to the idea of organizing Latino workers again. Public outrage began to grow, and union leaders were moved by the deplorable conditions that farmworkers were working under. In 1959, the AFL-CIO launched the Agricultural Workers Organizing Committee (AWOC), a new union organizing project. It was led by Mexican American Dolores Huerta and Filipino American Larry Itliong. Its goal was to organize the diverse farmworker labor force, which included large numbers of Latino and Asian workers. It was also planned as a cross-border organization, which set it apart from other labor unions who wanted to close the borders to immigrant workers.

As all of this was happening, Moreno continued to speak. News of her victory reached AWOC, who became very interested in this powerful woman. AWOC director Norman Smith, who had been an auto workers organizer in the 1930s and 1940s, reached out to Moreno with a job offer. She accepted, becoming the first Latina farmworker in U.S. history to be hired as a union organizer. Making history was nice, but Maria was more interested in results.

She immediately got to work. "Our only option is to get organized," she said in Spanish during a meeting. "Like it or not, we've got to struggle, and we won't stop fighting until we've won."

Moreno became a respected and effective messenger for the union. When she spoke, people listened—and sometimes, they cried. She lifted up her fellow farmworkers with as much conviction as when she gave speeches to politicians and university students. Laurie Coyle, producer of the 2018 documentary *Adios Amor: The Search for Maria Moreno*, described her as "a crusader in rubber boots and a big skirt." It was still unusual for a woman to be in Maria's position—traveling around organizing workers and speaking out in public—but many people appreciated her honesty. She gained a reputation as an engaging, charismatic, often blunt public speaker. That didn't mean she was popular with everyone in the movement. She famously butted heads with fellow farmworker organizer César Chávez, who grumbled that she had a "big mouth." He also disagreed with her about immigration; as a migrant worker who had spent her life on the road, Maria supported open borders. Some union leaders also disliked her organizing style, which focused on a bottom-up, worker-led approach. They were used to cutting backroom deals with employers. Maria was much more likely to set up a picket line and make the fight public.

In addition, AWOC had trouble getting enough funding. AFL-CIO president George Meany was not very enthusiastic about the project, and thought that they called too many strikes and used up too many resources. Their shoestring budget kept things running, but only just. Then, in 1960, disaster struck when the union ran into legal trouble. AWOC had put on a public screening of *Poverty in the Valley of Plenty*, a 1948 film about a contentious 1947 strike. During the strike, a massive agricultural company, DiGiorgio Fruit, had fired strikers and illegally hired replacement workers. DiGiorgio hated the film so much that they sued the filmmakers for libel, forcing them to destroy every copy of the movie. A handful of copies survived, though, which is how AWOC was able to screen the film for its members. Once they found out, though, DiGiorgio sued *them* for libel. An exasperated Meany pulled the plug on AWOC's funding, which left Maria and her fellow organizers scrambling for a solution. It was decided that they would send a delegation to the 1961 AFL-CIO convention in Miami, Florida. They held out hope that Maria could convince the other delegates to reverse Meany's decision.

At the convention, she spoke from the same stage as leaders like President John F. Kennedy, Martin Luther King Jr., Eleanor Roosevelt, and Walter Reuther. By all accounts, Maria gave an incredible performance. She used her time to describe the desperate conditions under which she and her children labored—the starvation, the poverty, the lack of healthcare. She called on the labor movement to stand with the farmworkers as they struggled to organize. She emphasized that, without their support, AWOC and the farmworkers would not be able to fight back against exploitation in the fields. They needed the full power of the labor movement behind them to bring the agricultural giants to heel. "Don't you think that our children had their stomachs full like the rest of you people that have a union or a decent wage?' she asked the crowd forcefully, reminding them of what her own children had undergone. "We don't. I hope that you people help us."

The plan worked. Maria's words had moved them, and the delegates voted overwhelmingly to reinstate support for the AWOC. However, their win was not unconditional. There were strings attached to that funding, and those who disliked AWOC used the opportunity to make some changes. AWOC was forced to reorganize their leadership structure ... and Maria lost her job. "She wasn't afraid to say whatever she had to say, whether it was a politician or a worker or whatever," farmworker organizer Gilbert Padilla explained in *Adios Amor*. "And I assume that's why they got rid of her."

Padilla went on to cofound the Farm Workers Association with fellow organizers César Chávez and Dolores

Huerta in 1962, which would evolve into the United Farm Workers (UFW). The UFW grew into a powerhouse and has built upon AWOC's work to become the mighty force for justice it still is today. Unfortunately, Moreno herself wouldn't be there to see it. When her former coworkers César and Dolores began organizing under the UFW name, Maria might have expected them to offer her a job working with them—but that call never came.

After being let go from AWOC, she left California and stepped away from the labor movement. Her heart was broken. It must have been so painful for her to have spent so much time, energy, and passion working as an organizer and fighting for her fellow farmworkers, only to be cast aside. Her strength and experience had been an invaluable tool, yet some of the men she worked with just couldn't handle the idea of taking orders from a woman.

So, at age 42, Maria took her life in a different direction entirely. The desire to help people remained, but her time in labor had bruised her, and she turned inward. She moved around the Southwest, eventually settling in Arizona. There, she became a Pentecostal preacher, and dedicated the rest of her life to religion. It made sense; her father had been a Baptist minister. Faith had always formed the bedrock of Maria's commitment to bettering the lives of others. She later founded a mission in Mexico where she and her family ministered to the poor until her death from breast cancer in 1989.

Maria Moreno left behind her beloved children, 46 grandchildren, 29 great-grandchildren, and an immortal legacy of resistance. "I've been a worker all my life," she loved to say. "I know how to handle a man's job like a man, and I'm not ashamed to say it. I'm an American citizen, and I'm talking for justice."

Ah Quon McElrath
The Island Uniter
1915–2008

Look, you are exploited, what are you going to do about it?

Ah Quon knew that she had to be blunt. She was in a union meeting full of workers who were upset and nervous. Tensions were high, and she needed to make sure her message was understood. There was no time to sugarcoat: they were in the middle of organizing a strike. Some of the workers were Native Hawaiians, but most were immigrants from countries like China, Japan, Korea, the Philippines, and Portugal. The one thing they all had in common was that they worked on the island's vast sugarcane plantations. Ah Quon was very familiar with how unfair the system was to workers of color, and those workers were getting ready to launch a major action to change it. Her nerves jangling, the short, serious Chinese Hawaiian woman turned to the crowd. "You are all economically exploited, whether you are Japanese, Chinese, Filipinos or whatever it is," she told them firmly. "What are you going to do about it?"

The United States government had annexed the independent nation of Hawai'i in 1898 and ruled it as a colony until it was formally made a state in 1959. During that time, American businessmen treated the islands like their own personal piggy bank. It took repeated mass action from the sugarcane plantation workers to even begin to level the playing field. The islands' first strike took place in 1900, and many more followed. In 1909, 5,000 Japanese workers went on strike for three months. That strike failed because plantation owners hired Chinese, Korean, Portuguese, and Hawaiian workers to cross the picket line, and paid them double their usual rate to take over the strikers' jobs. That disappointing experience taught both the bosses and the workers an important lesson. The plantation managers realized that pitting workers against one another based on their race and ethnicity could keep them from joining forces to protest the bosses' cruel, unfair policies. And the workers realized that the only way they could build enough power to beat the bosses was by putting their differences aside and working together as one.

Ah Quon was very familiar with these lessons by the time she became involved with the sugarcane workers. She also knew a little something about hard work. Her birth name was Leong Yuk Quon but she was better known by her nickname, Ah Quon. She had been born into poverty in O'ahu in 1915, and her parents, Leong

Chew and Leong Wong See, both immigrated there from Zhongshan, China. Her father worked as a contract laborer but died when Ah Quon was only four years old. Her mother was left to support their large family on her own. Everyone had to pitch in, including all seven children. For many years, Ah Quon and her siblings worked in a pineapple cannery after school and on weekends. Whenever she could find the time to study, she excelled. She was a star student and graduated from the University of Hawai'i in 1938 with a degree in sociology. Her early experiences with loss and deprivation fueled her ambition to help other people in tough situations. It's no surprise that as soon as she got to college, she joined several activist groups. She also became friends with Jack Hall, the president of the International Longshore and Warehouse Union (ILWU) Local 142 and helped him run the organizing newsletter *Voice of Labor*.

Ah Quon had wanted to pursue an advanced economics degree, but a trusted professor convinced her not to try. She had come to him for advice, hoping that he would steer her right. But instead, he insisted it would be too difficult for her because she was a woman and a person of color. He assumed she couldn't handle the mental exertion of higher education. It was an ugly betrayal. Stung by his bigotry and discouraged by his words, Ah Quon decided to take a different path. Drawing on her sociology background, she became a social worker. She got a job working with Hawai'i's Department of Public Welfare in 1939. Her friend Jack Hall introduced her to a union organizer named Bob McElrath, and two years later, the two of them married.

The young couple shared a deep interest in labor and a strong commitment to justice. Their partnership was built on a desire to make the world a better place. Labor was a natural home for them both, and they worked together to organize tuna packers, steamship workers, and pineapple canners (which must have felt very personal to Ah Quon). After World War II ended in 1945, they also became involved in the ILWU alongside their matchmaking friend, Jack. After years of inactivity, the islands' labor movement needed to make up for lost time. "I was involved in that early organizing of the longshoremen and then the war broke out. When the war broke out, almost nothing occurred," she told journalist Robynn Takayama in an interview. Once it was over, though, Ah Quon and her friends started making plans to take on the sugar barons who controlled the islands' agricultural economy.

The "Big Five" sugar companies—Alexander & Baldwin, American Factors, Castle & Cooke, C. Brewer, and Theo. Davies—ruled over Hawai'i's agricultural workforce with a level of control almost unimaginable today. The Hawaiian Sugar Planters' Association, as the Five's organizing cartel was known, employed more than one-fifth of the state's population. To the people living and working in Hawai'i, though, it seemed like they owned everything and everyone. The plantation bosses initially hired Native Hawaiians to work their fields, but soon decided it was easier to exploit vulnerable immigrant workers instead. They started importing laborers from China, then expanded to Japan, Korea, Portugal, the Philippines, Puerto Rico, and as far as Norway and Russia. In 1901, 200 Black workers were shipped in from Tennessee. The fields were full of a diverse group of workers from all around the world, but they were all paid too little and worked too hard. Once the workers arrived, the plantation bosses controlled everything about their lives. A 1939 report for the Bureau of Labor Statistics said, "The position of the individual plantation worker is especially vulnerable. The house in which he lives, the store from which he buys, the fields in which he finds his recreation, the hospital in which he is treated, are all owned by plantation management."

In 1944, the Big Five recruited 6,000 new laborers from the Philippines to join the existing majority Japanese workforce. During World War II, Japan and the Philippines were enemies. The bosses thought that the lingering political divide would keep those two groups of workers apart in the fields, too. It seemed like a foolproof plan. After all, pitting different groups of workers against one another had worked just fine before! But when the union found out about the plantation owners' plan, they made arrangements of their own. The ILWU wasn't just active in Hawai'i; they had members all over the West Coast and throughout the Pacific. It was time to get creative. So, they sent union organizers to take jobs as cooks and stewards aboard ships sailing from the Philippines to Hawai'i. It was their job to organize the new field workers before they could be used to break up the coming strike. Once the Filipino workers heard the whole story, it was an easy sell. By the time stewards aboard a ship docked on January 30, 1946, all the Filipino workers on board had already joined the ILWU. The union joyfully welcomed them with a brass band. "When those employers saw those [union] buttons, man, their faces dropped a foot-and-a-half, you know?" union organizer Frank Thompson later recalled. "So then we raised a lot of hell because the accommodations the planters had for these people were the same as you'd do cattle, only worse."

The ILWU had successfully given those workers the protection of a union before they stepped foot on Hawaiian soil. Ensuring that they felt welcome and allied with the union also meant that they wouldn't be easily pulled away by the bosses. While the ILWU was bringing workers into the union, the plantation bosses were trying to keep them out. With another big strike brewing, the union knew they had to do something different if they wanted to win this time.

Luckily, the workers had realized that the only way they could build enough power to beat the bosses was by working together. The ILWU hatched a plan that was very simple, and very effective: build strong bonds between the workers by treating everyone as equals. The union identified strong community leaders within each ethnic or racial group and involved them in strike planning. They held meetings in a variety of workers' languages like Japanese, Iloco, Tagalog, and Vasaya. The union set up two dozen strike kitchens and had different groups of workers cook for one another and share food. Most importantly, they put a strong emphasis on multiracial, multiethnic solidarity. As Ah Quon told them, it didn't matter where they'd come from or what language they spoke: they were all workers, and they had to fight, together.

Their efforts paid off. On September 1, 1946, about 26,000 sugar workers and their families, 76,000 people in all, walked out of the fields and went on strike. The workers stayed united. The bosses had hoped that workers who were newer to the plantations would not support the strike, but they were wrong. No one was willing to betray his fellow workers. "The Filipino workers who started working on the sugar plantations said look, we went through several years of extreme privation in the

Philippines—we lived in the mountains, we ate roots, we ate whatever insects we could catch, and if we were to go on strike here, we can live the same kind of life as we did in the Philippines," Ah Quon said in an interview about the strike. "Our membership was largely Japanese and a lot of them were in positions of leadership because by that time the Japanese were about 40 percent of the total population. [The Filipino workers] said it makes no difference to us, we are on strike, we will fight together."

The strike lasted for three months and shut down 33 of the 34 sugar plantations in the islands for 79 days. It also cost the Big Five over $15 million (about $241 million in 2024 dollars). Best of all, the workers won. They got a higher wage increase than they'd achieved in the past 20 years. They also won other demands like sick pay and an end to company-controlled housing, company-run medical care, and company-provided fuel. The strike also brought the workers more independence. "We were treated as human beings probably for the first time in our lives; we had a certain amount of equality with them," Ah Quon said.

And they had won because they stuck together and had each other's backs. "It didn't make a difference whether you were Filipino, Japanese, Chinese, or whatever it is, they felt that the strike had to be won and they gave their all in order to win the strike," Ah Quon said looking back on the victory. "And for me, this was a magnificent illustration of how people of different colors got together and worked to win the strike."

That victory was just the beginning, for Ah Quon at least. Ah Quon would be involved in many other strikes and campaigns throughout her long career as a social worker and labor organizer. In 1949, longshoremen struck over unequal pay; white workers on the mainland were being paid more than native Hawaiian and Asian immigrant workers. Once again Ah Quon stepped up to organize soup kitchens and help workers with paperwork. During that strike, she and the workers were loudly harassed by a group called We, the Women. This was an anti-labor group founded by Republican Ruth Black in response to the 1946 strike. The group recruited white housewives and professional women from elite families to loudly protest outside the ILWU offices and disrupt picket lines. They wanted to chip away at community support for the striking workers and force out the union's leaders, who they decided were too "radical."

Ah Quon was one of the people they targeted. She was a longtime member of the Communist Party. In the 1940s and 1950s, she was blacklisted from the Department of Social Security and was surveilled by the FBI. She was also subpoenaed by the House Un-American Activities Committee (HUAC) twice. She refused to apologize for her politics or to back down when pressured. She was tough and knew that she had done nothing wrong. All she wanted to do was organize and help people. The union stood by her and refused to give in to outside political pressure. They knew how important her work was and how much of an impact she had made.

In 1954, the ILWU hired her as a full-time social worker. During the 25 years she worked at the union, Ah Quon focused on community organizing and advocating for labor, women's, and immigrants' rights locally and on a state level. She led educational programs and helped union members and their families access government benefits. Outside of her official duties, she was also a trusted advisor to many of the union's leaders. They valued her knowledge, experience, and empathy—the same "radical" qualities that once got her targeted by the FBI! Ah Quon also stayed active politically in her local community. She pushed for social welfare legislation, local infrastructure projects, and universal healthcare programs, and won lower housing costs for workers. She never stopped learning, either. In 1965, she went to study at the Michigan School of Social Work, then spent three months working on a federally funded healthcare project for the Office of Economic Opportunity program at the Tuskegee Institute in Alabama. It was a very different environment from what she was used to at home in Hawai'i' and opened her eyes to new possibilities for worker education. Even after she retired from the union in 1981, Ah Quon refused to stop fighting. She was invited back to her alma mater to serve on the University of Hawai'i's Board of Regents and was awarded an honorary doctorate in 1988.

The honors were nice to have, but she knew her most important legacy would be with the people she left behind. She spent the rest of her life advocating for and organizing on behalf of the poor, the elderly, and the vulnerable. Growing up in poverty, organizing exploited agricultural workers, and helping union members navigate complicated systems had shaped her entire worldview. Ah Quon never lost faith in her vision of a strong and united multiracial, multiethnic, liberated working class. As she once warned, "The minute the trade union movement leaves out the word 'movement,' and thinks only of where it is going for itself, forget it, it ain't going anywhere." After nearly a century of hard work, Ah Quon died in 2008 at the age of 92.

Sue Ko Lee
The Voice of History
1910–1996

The strike was the best thing that ever happened. It changed our lives.

In the late 1980s, when historian Judy Yung decided she wanted to research a specific Chinese garment workers' strike, she knew that her first step would be trying to track down the workers who'd been involved. After all, the workers' voices are always the most important part of any labor story! There was one small problem though: that strike had happened in 1938, almost 50 years before Judy began looking into it. Most of the main players were already gone. This is one of the hard parts of writing about history—you never know if you're going to be too late. Judy did have to work extra hard to find anyone who had been involved, but finally she got lucky. She came across a woman named Sue Ko Lee, who had played an important role in the strike. Sue agreed to talk to her about what had happened back in the 1930s. By then, she was 79 years old, but she still had a lot to say about the strike, and all the things that led up to the moment when she and her coworkers walked out.

Sue Ko Lee told Judy about how she was born in Honolulu, Hawai'i, in 1910 and spent her childhood in Watsonville, California. It was a rural area in Santa Cruz County that depended mainly on agriculture, where many Chinese men were hired to work in the fields. Sue was the oldest of 10 children, so she probably learned pretty early what it was like to take care of other people. Watsonville had a thriving Chinatown, too, so she grew up surrounded by a close-knit community of both immigrants and American-born Chinese like herself. It helped her develop a strong sense of self, plus an independent streak. When she was 18, she met Lee Jew Hing, a young man who had emigrated from China. They soon married and settled in San Francisco. They quickly had two sons of their own, Mervyn and Stanley. Now that Sue had a growing family of her own to feed, she decided it was time to find a job.

Lee Jew Hing worked as a bookkeeper for National Dollar Stores, a Chinese American chain of dry goods stores. As a way to keep their prices low, most of the merchandise was made in a company-owned factory in San Francisco. The owner, Joe Shoong, only hired Chinese and Chinese American workers to work in his stores and factories. He was an important businessman who was respected by much of the community. He would eventually become one of the country's first Chinese American millionaires, but unfortunately, he did not share that wealth with the workers. They were paid very low wages and worked long hours in hot, unventilated, dirty sweatshops straight out of the early 1900s. Lee put in a good word for Sue Ko Lee, and she got a job in the factory as a buttonhole machine operator. She and her coworkers were paid only 25 cents an hour.

It was far from her dream job, but Sue had few other options. In the 1930s, Chinese and Chinese American workers still faced a huge amount of racism and prejudice in the U.S. That discrimination went back decades. The Chinese Exclusion Act, a law that forbade Chinese people from immigrating to the U.S., had been passed in 1882. It was a negative reaction to the first wave of Chinese workers who had traveled from their homeland to work on American railroads, mines, and farms. Major labor unions had publicly supported the law because they thought Chinese workers would take work away from their white members. In fact, decades after the law's passage, most white-owned companies would still not hire Chinese workers at all. Sue and her neighbors in San Francisco had no choice but to take whatever work they could in the city's Chinatown. About half of the neighborhood's total population worked in San Francisco's garment factories, including multiple generations of families. The lack of opportunities kept many of these workers poor and miserable, but what could they do?

In 1935, though, the landscape changed. That year, President Franklin D. Roosevelt implemented the New Deal, a series of social and economic reforms and programs with major input from the secretary of labor, Frances Perkins. One of the New Deal's major achievements was establishing a national minimum wage and protecting the right to unionize. As a result, labor unions began organizing more workers to build greater power. Union membership exploded during that time. Some of those unions also started reaching out to workers in the Black, Latino, and Asian communities that they had previously ignored. They realized that it made far more sense to add to their own numbers than to try and keep new people out. Their leaders still worried that bosses could use non-union workers of color to take work away from white members, but recruiting those workers into their own unions would at least keep them from becoming competition. For example, the International Ladies' Garment Workers' Union (ILGWU), which represented thousands of white women garment workers in other cities, thought that organizing Chinatown's garment factory workers would be a good way of raising standards across the industry. Of course, if it helped prevent Chinatown factory bosses from undercutting their white competitors, so much the better. "The white shops were already organized and they were clamoring that the contractors were sending work out to the Chinese workers," Sue Ko Lee explained. "So they had to organize the Chinese."

But it was not that simple. The ILGWU was sending its organizers into a community that spoke a different language and had different cultural customs and ideas about work. On top of that, those workers had a very understandable mistrust of unions. Why were these organizers coming into their neighborhoods *now*, when they'd been dealing with awful working conditions for decades? The Chinatown community was also deeply interconnected, and some workers did not want to damage their relationships with their employers by causing trouble. "First, they were afraid of their parents," one Chinese student named Chih Ling explained to Rose Pesotta, an organizer for the ILGWU. "Second, in nearly every instance most of the employees in the Chinese contracting factories were kin of the owner, regarded him as a benefactor, and would not go against his wishes. Third, they would lose their jobs, and probably would never be able to get others."

The stakes for organizing were very high for Chinese and Chinese American workers. After Pesotta published an article about Chinatown's "subterranean sweatshops," as she called them, inspectors came in and shut several of the factories down. It was not a popular move. The union didn't win many friends by bringing negative public attention to Chinatown. Factory owners lost money, and workers lost out on wages. The ILGWU made very little progress there until 1938, when it brought in a Hungarian American organizer named Jennie Maytas. As an immigrant herself and a former child garment worker, she was better equipped to navigate the delicate cultural and social environment of the Chinatown community. She was finally able to connect and build trust with the Chinese women who labored in the cramped garment factories. Her message to the workers was clear: "The Chinese garment workers live in poverty and insecurity not because they are Chinese, but because they still work under a system in which each stands weak and alone," she wrote in a letter to the editor of the *Chinese Digest*. "The International Ladies' Garment Workers' Union not only 'permits,' but pleads with Chinese garment workers to join our organization, to help abolish low wages and cutthroat labor competition."

Jennie's words resonated with the workers. "Why do we join the union? Improve the lives of workers, and eliminate unequal treatment," one pro-union flyer read. It still felt risky, but the union had proven that it actually cared about helping them. The factory women discussed it among themselves. They decided to take the plunge later that year. Sue Ko Lee and her coworkers voted to join the ILGWU, forming their own union within it, the Chinese

Ladies' Garment Workers' Union, Local 341. It was the first union of its kind, focused specifically on the needs of Chinese and Chinese American women in the garment industry.

At first, it seemed as though the company would be willing to cooperate with the union. It was an encouraging start to what the workers hoped would be an easy process. They held several promising bargaining sessions with National Dollar Stores management, and even came to a preliminary agreement on improving working conditions and raising wages to $20 per 35-hour week. But soon after, Shoong unexpectedly sold the factory to Golden Gate Manufacturing. It looked awfully like the company was trying to break the union and avoid giving the workers what they had promised.

Despite the betrayal, the workers sought a resolution. They were happy to have the ILGWU's support, but they had to be practical. Many of them used their wages to support their families, and they still needed to pay their bills. So the Chinese Ladies' Garment Workers' Union met with the National Dollar Store bosses and asked them to promise that they would buy their merchandise from the Golden Gate Manufacturing Company. That way, the workers could count on some stability. They wanted some guarantee that the factory would stay in business and their jobs would not disappear. Many garment workers in San

Francisco were at risk of losing their employment unexpectedly. Because there was so much competition, factories frequently went out of business, leaving the workers with nothing. The proposed arrangement would give them some peace of mind. But the bosses were angry that the workers had unionized and wanted to punish them for it. They refused to agree to their plan. Once again, they'd tossed aside the workers' concerns. The women were left with no other choice but to fight back.

On February 26, 1938, the Chinese Ladies' Garment Workers' Union went on strike. At eight a.m. sharp, more than 150 Chinese and Chinese American women workers of all ages walked out of the factory. They set up picket lines in front of the factory and at three National Dollar Store locations around the city. Their strike was the first organized labor action in San Francisco's Chinatown, and it was led by women like Sue Ko Lee. She and her coworkers rallied the strikers with speeches, led the picket lines, and even brought coffee and doughnuts for breakfast. It was an exciting time, but not everyone was on their side. Sue told Judy Yung that they did not receive much support from the Chinatown community. The women were called troublemakers. The National Dollar Store boss even tried to turn the local media against them. But as Sue said, "We knew the union was behind us."

As the weeks stretched on, it became difficult for the

strikers to make ends meet. The union gave them strike relief pay, but that only came out to five dollars a week. One worker, Edna Lee, told Jennie Maytas that the local grocers would not let her buy food on credit anymore, so she simply went hungry. The workers took care of one another and relied on their families to get by. The strike went on for 13 weeks—"Three and a half months!" Sue remembered. The tipping point came when the white clerks who worked at National Dollar Stores refused to cross their picket line. The ILGWU had contacted their union, the Retail Department Store Employees' Union. With no clerks, the stores could not remain open. Shoong finally had to act—and he responded by taking the union to court. Instead of negotiating with the workers, he sued the ILGWU and the Retail Employees' Union for $500,000 in damages. He also got a restraining order, and the workers had to stop picketing at three of his stores. They continued to make themselves heard outside the factory, though, and showed him and the other bosses that they would not give up.

Finally, on June 8, 1938, an agreement was reached. The strike had lasted 105 days, the longest in San Francisco history at that point. And in the end, the workers won! The new one-year union contract included a 5-percent raise; a 40-hour workweek; union recognition and representation; the enforcement of health, fire, and sanitary standards; a paid holiday on Labor Day; and more. The company also agreed to continue buying at least some of its merchandise from the Golden Gate Manufacturing Company. And Shoong dropped his lawsuits against the unions.

The ILGWU and Jennie encouraged the workers to accept the contract, but some members felt that it was not good enough. They had fought so hard and for so long, and were still not being paid what they were worth. Sue Ko Lee understood how they felt but urged her coworkers to be practical. It had already been a long three months. She knew all too well that none of them had unlimited resources, and neither did the union. "You have to start someplace," she told them. "At least you got something for one year. And maybe something better would come out of it. If you take longer, people are not going to stand around here. They can't afford to."

Ultimately, the contract was voted in. It was a close vote, with 31 workers voting for it and 27 against it, but as Sue Ko Lee said, it was a start. The workers found solace in the thought that they'd have the opportunity to improve upon it in their next contract. Armed with the new agreement, the women went back to work a few days later. The company held up their end of the bargain, too . . . at least until that first contract ran out. Then, suddenly, National Dollar Stores decided to start buying all of its merchandise elsewhere, and the Golden Gate Manufacturing Company went out of business. It was the exact scenario that the workers had tried to avoid. They would not get their chance to negotiate a better contract, either, because now they were out of a job.

They still had the union, though, and the ILGWU did not abandon its Chinese members. After the Golden Gate Manufacturing Company shut down, Jennie helped Chinese Ladies' Garment Workers' Union members find jobs in white-owned factories outside Chinatown. In doing so, those workers broke down the racial barrier that had long prevented them from finding work outside their neighborhood. "The door opened, and employers began asking for Chinese workers," Sue told Judy Yung. The white-owned factories paid more, too, so the workers also benefited economically. Sue Ko Lee and her husband both found work in white-owned union shops, where they made more money and got vacation time, stable work schedules, and health benefits. "In my opinion, the strike was the best thing that ever happened," Sue said. "It changed our lives. I know it was a turning point in my life."

She and other Chinese and Chinese American garment workers also took leadership roles within their own union and supported union workers in other industries. Sue stayed active in the ILGWU, putting her experience and pragmatism to use. She became secretary of its Local

101 while she was still working as a machine operator, and later became ILGWU's first Chinese American business agent. She was also a delegate for the ILGWU San Francisco Joint Board and attended national union conventions. After leaving the factory, Sue went to work for the union full-time. She worked as an organizer for the next 20 years. In the 1960s, she switched gears and went to work for the state of California's employment services. After she retired, Sue Ko Lee lived a quiet life in El Cerrito, California, until she died in 1996 at the age of 86.

During the 1938 strike, Sue had carefully saved many newspaper articles, letters, and photos in a scrapbook. Much of what we now know about the strike comes directly from her own memories and her interviews with Judy Yung. It is a precious gift to today's workers, who can look back and see themselves in Sue and her fellow garment workers' struggle—and see how far we have come. Without Sue Ko Lee's foresight, this important story might have been lost. And without the bravery, strength, and resilience she and her coworkers showed in the face of adversity, it wouldn't have happened at all.

Maida Springer Kemp
The Globe-Trotting Organizer
1910–2005

I have an unending love affair with the American labor movement.

It was a hot August day on Ellis Island in 1917, and Maida was very far from home. It was an overwhelming scene, full of unfamiliar voices. Everywhere she turned, there were people. Families carrying bags and boxes, tired parents shepherding their children, and, most intimidatingly, the immigration officers questioning people as they stood in a long line. Maida and her family had just stepped off the big ship that had brought them from Panama to the United States. Their journey had been long, but tolerable; unlike the poorer passengers in steerage, her family had been able to afford to travel in relative comfort. When they arrived at the immigration processing center on Ellis Island, though, Maida and her family became just another group of faces in the crowd. She was seven years old, with big, curious brown eyes and a shy smile. She held her mother Adina's hand and watched as she helped other Spanish-speaking people communicate with the American officials. It seemed as if they'd been in line forever, but little did Maida know that her journey had only begun.

Maida's family ended up in Harlem, a neighborhood in the northern end of New York City that was home to a great many Black residents. They were part of a large migration of Caribbean people who emigrated to the U.S. between 1900 and 1930. Their new neighborhood was alive with familiar Caribbean sounds and smells, but they were not the only cultural group who called Harlem home. Black immigrants from Central America and South America joined those who came from the American South and elsewhere in the Caribbean. Harlem evolved into a major center of Black culture. Maida was happy to meet people from all over and learn from her mother's friends in the political community. Her new world wasn't entirely perfect, though. The pressures of building a new life from scratch had led to her parents' marriage dissolving soon after they arrived. Her father was soon gone, leaving her mother to look after the children herself.

Adina became involved in the movement for African liberation and a member of the Universal Negro Improvement Association (UNIA). Maida listened closely as the adults discussed concepts like colonialism, racism, and self-determination. She took the lessons they taught her to school, where she had to endure racism, discrimination, and cruel taunts from both her teachers and her classmates. The other students made fun of how she spoke (her first language was Spanish), how she looked, and where she came from. Her white teachers bullied and disrespected her. Her mother, frustrated with the way the New York City schools were failing her daughter, started looking into alternatives.

Adina found a boarding school in Bordentown, New Jersey, staffed by Black teachers; it sounded just right. Maida was relieved to feel like less of an outsider, but she still found it difficult to fit in. Outside school, she tried her best to help her mother pay the bills, but that was hard, too. When she was only 11, she tried to get a job with the New York Telephone Company but was rejected ... not because of her age, but because of her skin color. It was something that would happen to her again and again as she made her way through the American workforce.

Her mother held political gatherings in their apartment and took Maida along to meetings. She also gave her an early introduction to the labor movement by having her fold leaflets for a friend's father, who was in the all-Black Brotherhood of Sleeping Car Porters union. By the time she was a teenager, Maida had been given a thorough course in anti-Black racism and how it impacted the way she was able to move through the world.

When she was 17, Maida married Owen Springer, a Barbadian like her father. At first, she stayed home to take care of their children. But when the Great Depression hit,

Owen lost his job as a repairman and Maida had to go find work in the garment industry. She joined Local 22 of the International Ladies' Garment Workers' Union (ILGWU) in 1933, just in time for them to call a 60,000-strong dressmakers' strike. Maida was excited to join them. She called the strike "an electrifying occasion" and it inspired her to get more involved in the union. That same year, she went to see the Brotherhood of Sleeping Car Porters' president, A. Philip Randolph, give a speech. She was still a little distrustful of organized labor, which had its own reputation for anti-Blackness and racial discrimination. Randolph's speech changed her mind. He was able to connect the dots between how racist employers tried to divide workers and stop Black economic advancement. Maida, thinking of the discrimination she had already faced, came away dazzled by the potential of union power. "He excited my interest and challenged my mind to think about something besides the prejudice against the Black community," she later recalled. "I got a PhD education in survival from Randolph and an awareness of a struggle and of Black and white relationships." Randolph and Maida later became close friends.

Now that she finally felt like she fit in somewhere, Maida threw herself into the labor movement. She joined numerous committees and immersed herself in the union's robust educational offerings. Maida discovered that she was a natural leader and rose quickly through the union ranks. She was invited to join its executive board in 1938 and signed on as Local 22's educational director in 1943. It was an impressive achievement for someone so young.

Her husband wasn't as excited about it. He did not trust unions. He also wasn't very supportive of her career, which made Maida sad. She refused to give up, though, and continued to climb. She became the union's first Black business agent to lead an entire district and stayed in that role until 1959. Outside of her union work, she also juggled raising a family and continuing in her mother's tradition of political organizing. Owen never came around to her union work, and it would eventually lead to the breakdown of their relationship in 1955. Maida was heartbroken, but she could not share her life with a person who didn't support her mission or understand its importance.

Maida wasn't a political rebel, but her actions as an organizer were certainly radical for the Jim Crow era. This was a time when Black people were treated as second-class citizens and harshly denied many basic rights. It was extraordinary for someone like Maida to be as outspoken as she was, just like Lucy Parsons and many other women in this book so many years before. She was a tremendously strong person. No one could bully her into changing her mind or allowing racists, sexists, or colonizers to tell her who she was or how she should act. She was determined to achieve racial and economic justice for Black workers—and she wasn't interested in arguing. Maida also remained politically independent, which made her extra unique in her circles. In that era, many labor organizers and union members were involved in the Communist Party or interested in their political ideology. Throughout her early career with the ILGWU, internal arguments between Communists and anti-communists often caused issues within the union. While Maida appreciated the U.S. Communist Party's anti-racist stance, she didn't trust its motives. She felt that they were tokenizing her as a Black immigrant woman. "The thing that offended me was that I always felt that I was being patronized," she told Richards. "I think they loved me too much."

After spending 10 years at the ILGWU, Maida was given an exciting new opportunity to expand her work. In 1945, she was invited to join a delegation to England to meet with British and European labor leaders, visit factories, and observe wartime conditions. That trip marked the beginning of her international career as the first Black woman to represent U.S. labor overseas. It was also the first time she'd traveled across an ocean since she'd left her childhood home in Panama. It was an important mission that Maida did not take lightly. She was determined to learn as much as possible—and was surprised to see how familiar certain things felt. She may have left Jim Crow back in the U.S., but she was still expected to sleep in a separate room from her white fellow delegates.

In London, Maida met with African and Caribbean soldiers, who told her stories from the front lines of the fight for colonial independence. Seeing the battle through their eyes was thrilling and hardened her resolve to continue pushing forward. She connected with Trinidadian pan-Africanist socialist George Padmore, who would become her lifelong friend and mentor, and Jomo Kenyatta, an anti-colonial activist who would become the first president of an independent Kenya. When she met him, Jomo asked her, "Young girl, what does the working class in America know of the struggle for liberation from colonialism?" That question changed the course of her life. From that moment on, she became determined to convince U.S. labor leaders to support both the African struggle for independence and a strong democratic labor movement.

During the 1950s and 1960s, Maida formed deep connections with labor leaders and anti-colonial activists in multiple African countries. Her first trip to Africa came in 1955, and took her to Accra, Ghana. She was there for work, but found some time to drink it all in. There, she served as an AFL observer and delegate to an International Confederation of Free Trade Unions (ICFTU) conference. It was a politically complex event, and the tension between different political groups made Maida feel as though she was "dancing on the end of a needle." Arguing at a stuffy convention wasn't her style. She tried to ignore the drama and focused instead on her plans to organize workers in newly independent African nations like Kenya, Nigeria, Tanzania (formerly Tanganyika), Uganda, and Ghana.

Her experiences varied from nation to nation. In most African countries, she was greeted warmly as "Mama Maida" and treated with respect. But when she visited Southern Rhodesia (now Zimbabwe), she was treated with outright hostility. Rhodesia was an apartheid state, and its society was explicitly white supremacist; Black residents were abused, criminalized, and treated as less than human. Maida's memories of growing up in the Jim Crow era were never that far away, and it must have been jarring to experience the same kind of ugly prejudice so far from her adopted home.

She often felt as though she was trapped between two worlds. While she had no problem connecting with workers, Maida's relationships with colonial government officials and her European colleagues were more difficult to navigate. They didn't always see her as a powerful labor leader; they just saw a Black woman who seemed way too confident and needed to be humbled. Maida took the disrespect in stride, but it must've been draining. She was often searched at the borders of colonized states, which added hours of unnecessary nonsense to her travels.

When she brought up the issue of racism with her European coworkers, they would quickly point to America's own problems with systemic racism to avoid discussing their own cultural failings. It was a source of endless frustration. Why couldn't they see that it was all connected?

In 1960, she joined the AFL-CIO's International Affairs Department as its representative to Africa. All her hard work was bearing fruit. Over the next five years, she witnessed independence celebrations in Nigeria, Tanzania, Gambia, and Kenya. She even found time to marry her second husband, James Horace Kemp, a well-respected Chicago labor organizer and activist who would later be elected president of the NAACP. He not only understood her commitment to labor, but he was also proud to be partnered with such an accomplished organizer. It was a happy time in Maida's life; she had already made labor history on her own, and now she had a new opportunity to continue doing the work she loved in a bigger way.

During Maida's time at the AFL-CIO, she took on organizing projects in multiple African countries. She devoted herself to organizing and funding educational opportunities for members of the African poor and working class in Tanzania, where she established a scholarship for girls' continuing education. In Kenya, she worked with the Kenya Tailors and Textile Workers Union and founded a trade school for women, raising funds to build Nairobi's

Solidarity House worker center. In Nigeria, she partnered with the Nigerian Motor Drivers' Union and secured AFL-CIO funding to establish a Motor Drivers' Driving School. At the urging of her friends in African labor, she and her old friend A. Philip Randolph founded an exchange program that enabled African worker centers to send their members to the Harvard Labor-Management Industrial Relations Center. Political disagreements and global conflicts often got in her way, but Maida refused to lose sight of her vision for international labor solidarity.

Maida would continue to work, organize, and advocate for African workers for the rest of her life, but she didn't forget about the U.S. In 1966, she returned to the ILGWU and began working as a general organizer for the union in the South. In 1970, she was asked to serve as the Midwest director of the A. Philip Randolph Institute, a racial and economic justice organization dedicated to strengthening ties between the labor and civil rights movements. During that same period, she began working with the African American Labor Center (AALC) to organize relief programs for drought-stricken Western and Central Africa nations. In 1973, she joined its staff full-time. She also became a consultant for the Asian-American Free Labor Institute and helped organize women workers in Turkey and Indonesia. Throughout these years, she was traveling to Africa and Europe for seminars and conferences, and working on events with the NAACP's Task Force in Africa. In her few free moments, she stayed active in numerous women's and civil rights organizations like the National Organization of Women (NOW), the Coalition of Labor Union Women (CLUW), the National Council of Negro Women, and the Urban League. It's a wonder she ever found time to sleep!

By the time she retired in 1981, Maida had received countless awards and recognitions, including an honorary doctorate from Brooklyn College. She also lived to see the establishment of the Maida Springer Kemp Fund, which worked to fight child labor in East Africa by creating opportunities for young people there. Maida's entire life was shaped by her experiences as a Black woman living at the intersection of labor, race, gender, class, and colonialism. Her incredible career is a beautiful reminder that the cause of labor is a global struggle.

Maida died in 2005 at the age of 84. She had achieved her dreams, and then some. "I have an unending love affair with the American labor movement," she once said. "To the degree that a government can be challenged and workers can have the right to help to determine their hours of work, conditions of employment, redress of their grievances, it's the labor movement that made this contribution on behalf of the working class. I remain a member of that class without apology."

Emma Tenayuca
Fighting for Justice

1916–1999

We can no longer wait for better days without fighting for those better days!

Emma Tenayuca was a born fighter. She was only a teenager when she began organizing workers in her hometown of San Antonio and would spend the entirety of her long life pushing back against those who wanted to silence or intimidate her. Emma's passion for the cause was legendary—it even gave her a famous nickname. She was an inspirational labor leader, an important part of Texas history, and a heroine to many. But before she was any of that, Emma Tenayuca was a working-class Mexican kid who took a look around and decided that things needed to change—and that she was going to be the one to change them.

Emma was born in San Antonio, Texas, on December 21, 1916. Her family struggled financially, so Emma was sent to live with her grandparents. She was very close with her grandfather, Francisco Zepeda, a carpenter who closely followed Mexican politics and supported Mexican independence. Much of her early education came directly from him. He taught young Emma, who was of Spanish and Comanche descent, about the impacts of racism on their community and about Mexican identity. He also took her to Plaza del Zacate in San Antonio's Milam Park, where they listened to activists talk about politics and workers' rights. The lessons Emma learned from her grandfather stayed with her as she grew. In high school, she joined the debate team and played sports . . . but she also joined a reading club that exposed her to the work of Karl Marx, Thomas Paine, and other radical thinkers. The seeds had been planted.

In 1933, Emma came across a group of Mexican women workers from the H. W. Finck Cigar Company who were striking over low wages and unsanitary working conditions. She knew that it was important to support strikers, and enthusiastically took her place marching beside them. Soon, the police arrived—and attacked. Emma was frightened and horrified to see how they treated the women she'd just befriended. She was arrested alongside the women workers and taken down to the police station. "I landed in jail and learned how difficult it would be to make this a union town," she remembered years later. Once he knew she was safe, her grandfather must have chuckled to himself as she told him all about her first experience walking on a picket line. He had taught her well. She was only 16, but Emma had already found her purpose.

The labor bug bit her hard. As soon as Emma graduated high school, she found a job as an elevator operator and became deeply involved in the local labor movement. She joined in on community organizing as well, helping to create connections between unions and Spanish-speaking workers. She was still in her late teens in 1934 and 1935, when she helped organize two locals of the International Ladies' Garment Workers' Union. It was an astounding achievement for such a young person, but Emma felt like she was only getting started.

It also provided a critical learning experience for the young organizer. After spending months trying to get the ILGWU to meet the workers where they were, Emma decided that the ILGWU leaders just weren't cut out to address the unique needs and culture of the Mexican American community. That lack of mutual understanding in turn created friction between her and the union leaders. Fed up with the whole situation, Emma left and directed her energy elsewhere. She joined a political group called the Young Communist League, and with their support, began organizing Mexican workers into Unemployed Councils. These councils were part of a broader Depression-era Communist Party program to mobilize the unemployed and educate them about communism. Emma appreciated the Communist Party's anti-racist, anti-sexist principles, and admired the successes of the Mexican Communist Party. She saw their political program as a means to organize the working class on a mass scale. "Communists were at the forefront of the struggle," she wrote later, and that's exactly where she wanted to be.

By the end of 1937, nearly everyone in San Antonio knew about Emma. She was a constant presence at rallies, demonstrations, and on picket lines, and devoted all of her time to helping exploited workers and unemployed people. Her rocky start in labor was forgotten and instead, she became known and respected for her organizing abilities. The passionate speeches she delivered earned her the nickname *La Pasionaria*—The Passionate One. "The time is now for the workers to organize!" she thundered to one crowd. "We can no longer wait for better days without fighting for those better days!" She had a sense of humor, too; she grew up during the Great Depression, and once told an interviewer that her biggest motivation was simple: "Food!"

The Unemployed Councils eventually combined forces with other leftist groups to form the Workers Alliance of America, and Emma became a member of its executive committee. She was also the general secretary for San Antonio's chapters, and represented 10,000 Workers Alliance members there. About 3,000 of those members worked in the city's pecan industry. Emma probably got to know some of them through her leadership role, but she would have been able to connect with them on a more personal level, too. Nearly all of them were women, and most of them shared the same working-class Mexican and Mexican American background that she did. They saw her as one of them.

In 1938, pecans were big business. Not only that, it was a near monopoly, as half of the country's entire pecan market was controlled by the Southern Pecan Shelling Company in San Antonio. Its owners, Julius Seligmann and Joe Freeman, had gotten rich off their system to "streamline" the labor-intensive process of shelling nuts. They sold their raw product to over 100 different contractors, who then farmed out the labor to predominantly Mexican and Mexican American workers. By distributing the labor this way, the owners were able to ignore labor regulations and avoid paying the workers fairly. Prior to 1926, pecan companies had used machines to handle most of the process, but Southern Pecan discovered it was cheaper to hire Mexican and Mexican American workers to shell the nuts by hand. "They did not go for machines, because they had such a large group of people here to exploit," Tenayuca explained to journalist Luis R. Torres in a 1987 interview.

And their exploitation was absolutely brutal. The

contractors paid men more than women, but all of the workers were paid very, very poorly. The average wage for a pecan worker was $2 to $3 per week. However, the most dangerous part of their jobs wasn't necessarily the terrible pay scale, it was the air they breathed—and more specifically, the pecan dust that floated through the stuffy factory and down into the workers' lungs. The factory was always dirty, and there was little ventilation. "They had to all sit together at this long table under very crowded conditions," University of Texas History Professor Gabriela Gonzalez told Texas Public Radio in 2018. "There was a lot of brown dust in the air from the pecan shelling that would get into the lungs. Some of these folks would end up with asthma, tuberculosis."

During this period, the rate of tuberculosis among San Antonio's pecan shellers was almost *three times* the national average. It's a shocking statistic that somehow didn't get anywhere near the attention it deserved at the time. To most Americans, the pecan shellers were invisible. Meanwhile, many of the workers took piles of pecans home with them to continue working after their shifts ended. Entire families would spend their nights cracking open as many nuts as possible. A contemporary study cited in Justin Akers Chacón's terrific *Radicals in the Barrio: Magonistas, Socialists, Wobblies, and Communists in the Mexican-American Working Class* described how "thousands of human beings living in decrepit wooden shacks or in crowded corrals breathlessly shelled pecans in a race with starvation." It was a recipe for suffering. By the time Emma got involved, a revolt was already brewing amid the brown dust and cracked shells.

While Emma had been busy organizing with the ILGWU, workers at the Southern Pecan Shelling Company went on strike in 1934, and again in 1935. They hadn't had the support of a union during those earlier actions, but that changed in 1937 when Congress of Industrial Organizations (CIO) organizers Minnie Rendón, Leandro Ávila, and Willie Garcia stepped in. With their help, the pecan shellers formed Pecan Workers Local 172. The union was officially chartered as part of the powerful United Cannery, Agricultural, Packing, and Allied Workers of America (UCAPAWA). Their timing couldn't have been better, either. In 1938, Southern Pecan infuriated the workers by slashing their already tiny paychecks. That was the last straw for many of them—and this time, they had a union to back them. On January 31, 1938, nearly 12,000 pecan shellers—the vast majority of them Mexican and Mexican American women—walked off the job. It would become the biggest strike in San Antonio's history.

The workers elected Emma to lead their strike committee. She was only 21, but they had been working alongside her for years by then. They trusted her to represent them fairly and fight for their interests. She eagerly accepted the role. The strike's first day was a pivotal moment for all of them ... and 24 hours later, Emma was in jail alongside several other organizers. Police had swooped in and broken up their picket line, just like she'd seen them do to the cigar workers all those years ago. The strike organizers were only freed after a crowd of 300 supporters surrounded the jail and demanded their release. This rude welcome from the city's power brokers was only the beginning of what would become a protracted battle. The striking workers quickly realized that they would have to take on not only the pecan kings, but also the mayor, the cops, the city's conservative Mexican middle class, and even the Church.

San Antonio's mayor Charles K. Quin was no fan of organized labor. He fumed as he watched the growing movement of disenfranchised, increasingly militant workers of color spread throughout his city. It really was the last thing he wanted to deal with at that moment, and maybe that was why he did what he did. His solution to the problem of the strike was creative, if not entirely logical: he simply decided to pretend it did not exist. Instead, he insisted that it was an attempted "revolution" that was being led by outsider political activists. In choosing to phrase it that way, Quin was attempting to ensure that the strike would not fall under the protections of the 1935 Wagner Act, which protects workers' right to collectively bargain. As far as he was concerned, this was not the action of a labor union; it was a rebellion.

Police Chief Owen Kilday followed Quin's lead. Armed with tear gas, riot gear, and lethal weapons, the San Antonio police force terrorized the striking workers. The repression went far beyond the actual picket line. The police disrupted the community's attempts to deliver supplies to the workers, shut down strike kitchens, and raided suspected strike leaders' homes. It seemed as though they wanted the strikers to starve, or at least to be on edge every moment of every day. Over 1,000 men, women, and children were arrested during the three-month conflict. When the arrestees sang songs of solidarity in their overcrowded cells, their jailers turned fire hoses on them. An investigation by the Texas Industrial Commission later found that the San Antonio police's interference with the strikers' right to peaceful assembly was unjustified. But the police faced no consequences for their behavior (and Kilday's brother, Paul, was later elected to the U.S. House of Representatives).

During the strike, Tenayuca and her fellow organizers endured months of criticism and threats from the Southern Pecan bosses as well as from local San Antonio business and religious leaders. By then, Emma was a member of the Communist Party. That gave her opponents more ammunition, and she was targeted for her political beliefs.

But instead of defending her, the CIO buckled under the pressure. They turned their backs on one of their most effective organizers. The CIO removed her position as strike leader, replacing her with CIO organizer J. Austin Beasley. When Beasley arrived in San Antonio, he immediately removed women from the strike's leadership. He depended on the Latina women organizers for guidance but refused to give them any power over their own strike. It was an ugly betrayal. Emma was furious, but she was not about to abandon the workers. She might have lost her public role, but was still able to provide support behind the scenes. As she wrote, "I continued to write all the circulars, [and] met with all the picket captains."

The strike dragged on. National media finally began to take note of all the mass arrests and police violence against the strikers. "These little brown women were being beaten by the police," Sarah Gould, lead curatorial researcher at the Institute of Texan Cultures, told the *Ranger* in 2017. "It got a lot of media coverage, and it brought a lot of attention to this kind of injustice." The pecan shellers became a national—and international—cause. Texas Governor James Allred informed the mayor that he supported the workers' right to peacefully picket. The Mexican Consul protested the arrests and jailing of dozens of Mexican citizens. Pressure built up for 37 days until the two parties agreed to participate in arbitration.

The negotiations ended with a win for the strikers. They would finally be paid a minimum wage and the company agreed to recognize their union. The Texas Industrial Commission also launched an investigation into the workers' grievances.

Though the strikers had won their battle against Southern Pecan, they didn't get to celebrate their victory for very long. When Congress passed the 1938 Fair Labor Standards Act later that year, it established a minimum hourly wage of 25 cents. Still smarting from losing the strike, Southern Pecans owners grumbled that paying the new standard wage would cut into their profits. They decided it was unfair to force them to pay their workers properly. The owners petitioned the government for an exception from the new law and shut down the pecan factories while they waited for a response. When the government denied their request, Southern Pecan's owners responded by bringing in the shelling machines they'd previously avoided—and laying off 10,000 pecan shellers. By 1948, Pecan Shelling Workers Union No. 172 had fully dissolved. Mechanization had taken over the pecan industry, leaving the workers to search for employment elsewhere. The pecan kings had sacrificed their entire workforce just to save a few cents per hour.

Emma herself wasn't there to see any of it unfold. Her ordeal in San Antonio had left her feeling tired and unwelcome, and all the negative press about her had made it difficult to find a job. She was left at loose ends. During World War II, she tried to join the Women's Auxiliary Air Corps but was rejected due to her Communist ties. Ironically, her own political sentiments soon shifted. Stalin's depraved actions during the war chipped away at her enthusiasm for the ideology that he embraced. By 1948, she had left both San Antonio and the Communist Party. Emma finally found some peace in San Francisco, where she spent the next 20 years raising a son and working as a teacher.

It took time for the scars to heal, but as the years went by, Emma yearned to return home. When she finally came back to Texas, it was to help educate the next generation of activists. As it turned out, things had changed quite a bit since she'd been, more or less, run out of San Antonio. When she left, she'd felt abandoned and unwanted; when she came back, she was greeted with open arms. It was a total reversal. "To my surprise," she said, "I return and I find myself some sort of a heroine."

Unbeknownst to her, during the 1970s, a whole new generation of labor, Chicano, and women's liberation activists had begun to rediscover her work. Emma became a hero to them and to many others who appreciated her determination and sacrifices. The honors began rolling in. She was inducted into the San Antonio Women's Hall of Fame in 1991. There are songs and murals dedicated to her memory, and she and the pecan strikers are featured in the 2018 documentary *A Strike and an Uprising in Texas*. In 2021, Virginia Hartung, a public history graduate student at St. Mary's University, circulated a petition to rename San Antonio's Beauregard Street—which currently honors a Confederate general—to Tenayuca Street.

"She was really kind of written out of history," her niece, San Antonio attorney Sharyll Tenayuca, said during an event commemorating the strike's 84th anniversary. Those who opposed her views on working-class liberation hated and feared her. They had isolated her and tried to silence her. Unfortunately for them, there are still many people who remember Emma Tenayuca's life of militancy, mutual aid, and multiracial, multi-gender solidarity.

In the end, she won.

Emma Tenayuca died on July 23, 1999, but her story will never be forgotten. "I was arrested a number of times," she said in an interview in 1983, when she was 67 years old. "I don't think that I felt exactly fearful. I never thought in terms of fear. I thought in terms of justice."

Dorothy Bolden
Pride, Professionalism, and Progress
1924–2005

I organized to update the field, to make it more professional.

Dorothy sighed. It was another hot, humid day in Atlanta, Georgia, and the window was stuck. As she leaned back against the seat, she could feel the sweat dripping off her nose. It was still early in the morning, but the sun didn't care what the clock said. She was on her way to work, and the bus was packed with other domestic workers just like her. They spent their days performing household tasks like cooking, cleaning, scrubbing, ironing, and serving the wealthier families who hired them. It wasn't a coincidence that Dorothy and her fellow workers were all Black, while the families they worked for were white.

Atlanta in the 1930s was a very unequal place; Jim Crow was still alive and well, and Black people were discriminated against socially, politically, and economically. Both of Dorothy's parents worked hard jobs. Her father was a chauffeur, and like many Black working women at that time, Dorothy's mother brought in money by doing other people's laundry. Bundles of dirty clothes would appear at their home, and she'd spend hours scrubbing them clean. When Dorothy was small, she would help by delivering the fresh clothes back to her mother's clients. And when it came time for Dorothy to get a job of her own, she became a domestic worker, too. She started working when she was only nine years old. Her first job was washing her mother's clients' dirty diapers.

It was not unusual then for a young Black girl like Dorothy to go to work. She did have a harder time of it than most other girls in her position, though, because Dorothy was visually impaired. She had an accident when she was a toddler that damaged the nerves in her eyes. The doctor declared her legally blind. (He wasn't sure if she would ever see again, but her vision gradually improved as she got older.) No matter how cloudy her vision was, there were bills to pay and younger siblings to feed. Dorothy had to work. When she was in the 11th grade, she dropped out of high school to work full-time. She worked from early in the morning until evening and made $3 per week.

It was a difficult life. She dreamed of doing more, even as the odds were stacked against her. Her employers did not treat her with respect, and acted as though she and her fellow Black domestic workers were disposable. Dorothy knew better. Her mother had raised her to stand up for herself. When her white employer demanded that she work late one night, Dorothy refused the request. Shocked, her boss called the police. They just couldn't believe that a young Black woman would have had the audacity to talk back to a white woman. They actually questioned her sanity! That's how rare it would have been. She only avoided being locked up in a mental health facility because her uncle paid for a psychiatric evaluation that showed she was perfectly healthy. She was just tired of being treated poorly. That traumatizing experience only fueled her determination to keep pushing forward.

When she got older, Dorothy spent a brief amount of time at design school. Her eye problems made it too difficult for her to complete her schoolwork, though, so she couldn't continue going. After that, she tried out several other jobs in several other cities like Chicago, Illinois, and Detroit, Michigan. She also married, but that ended quickly. She sold shoes, was a restaurant worker, designed dresses, worked in a factory, and then got a job with National Linen Service, a linen supply company. There, she received her first taste of collective worker power. Her coworkers unionized during her time there, and Dorothy was amazed to see her daily wage rocket up from $3 to $23. She never forgot that feeling, and that moment taught her an important lesson about organizing.

Still, Dorothy kept coming back to domestic work.

Other opportunities were either scarce, or simply weren't a good fit. She took a great deal of pride in domestic work. She especially loved caring for her employers' children. It was so important to her that she would refuse to take jobs that didn't involve childcare. "A domestic worker is a counselor, a doctor, a nurse," Dorothy once said. "She cares about the family she works for as she cares about her own." When she and her second husband, Abraham Thompson, decided to start a family, it soon grew to include seven children. Dorothy would stay home with them when they were small, then head right back to work as soon as she could. With that many kids to feed, there wasn't much time to spare.

In 1955, Dorothy was watching television when she saw a woman named Rosa Parks on the news. The woman on the bus looked tired but proud, a feeling that Dorothy herself had felt a thousand times before as she made her way home from another long day at work. Rosa could have been her mother, or her aunt, or her. That image stuck with her. During the early 1960s, Dorothy became involved with the civil rights movement herself. She volunteered with the Student Nonviolent Coordinating Committee, an influential group of civil rights activists who opposed segregation and organized peaceful direct-action protests across the South. Its membership included politician icons like Ella Baker, Stokely Carmichael, Gloria Richardson,

John L. Lewis, and Dr. Martin Luther King Jr. "I marched with Dr. King every time he came to town," she recalled. "I went to rallies, I was the most vocal person there. I stayed that way and Dr. King sent SNCC and all the rest of them: 'Look Bolden up down there, she'll help you.'" In 1964, she organized her first political action, leading a boycott of Atlanta schools to protest the school board's refusal to treat Black students fairly.

Dorothy was also worried about the conditions she and her fellow domestic workers labored under. Their wages were still far too low, and it had an impact on more than just their pocketbooks. Dorothy was concerned about how their low wages impacted their ability to participate in the broader fight against segregation. Respectability was a big issue for her, and so was keeping up appearances. No matter how tired she was from work, she always ensured that she and her children were all neat, clean, and well-dressed whenever they went out. "We couldn't be going to integrate the schools out there barefooted," she explained in a 1995 oral history interview. "I didn't want to integrate my child into a society like that [if they] didn't have no shoes or decent clothes to put on." She thought back to her experience with the linen company and decided that the domestic workers needed a union.

In those days, Dr. King was her next-door neighbor on Auburn Avenue in Atlanta. They were friendly and she knew she could turn to him for advice. One day, when she asked him for ideas on how to organize domestic workers, he told her, "You do it—and don't let nobody take it. I know they will have a fight on their hands if they try to take it." He wasn't wrong! Dorothy took his advice and ran with it. She had been riding the bus to work since she was a child, so she knew that those hot, uncomfortable rides were often the only time that domestic workers had to talk amongst themselves. The rest of their workdays were spent in isolation, bending over other people's stoves or chasing their kids around. Bolden used the bus as her own personal mobile union hall.

She'd plunk down next to someone and strike up a conversation with her about wages, long hours, nasty employers, and aching bodies. The other women trusted her, because she was one of them. She knew the pain of a 13-hour day, the pinch of low wages, and the prickle of constant disrespect. Bolden traveled around the city, taking every bus line, trying to reach every worker she could. In addition to working conditions, voting rights were another huge issue for Dorothy—so she found a way to combine the two. In between bus trips and shifts at work, she helped run voter registration drives for domestic workers. "I don't want to be out here pushing for you and you not registered to vote," she told her members. "We aren't Aunt Jemima women, and I sure to God don't want people to think we are. We are politically strong and independent."

She also had to fend off harassment from the Ku Klux Klan, a racist terrorist group who would call her house and threaten her life. It was a very real danger. The Klan was and still is extremely violent, and especially hated outspoken Black civil rights activists. "I never told anybody because it didn't scare me, didn't bother me," she later said. "It made me angry, it made me determined to do what I had to do." The threats faded into the background whenever she got back to work. Dorothy poured as much energy into organizing as she could spare. As a mother of seven with a full-time job, it was quite a challenge. She did it anyway—and she had a plan to do even more.

In 1968, after getting a few last pieces of advice from trusted voices within the labor movement, Dorothy made her move. She put out a call on the radio and in Black-owned newspapers inviting domestic workers to the first meeting of the National Domestic Workers Union. By publicly announcing the new organization, she was willing her plan into motion. Eight women came to the first meeting, but many more followed. Unsurprisingly, Dorothy was elected the group's first president. There was one wrinkle: the Atlanta Urban League, a community organization, was also interested in organizing domestic workers. Dorothy had mentioned her project to them previously, but they hadn't given her the time of day. Now they were announcing a meeting of their own! When she heard about what the League was up to, she was more than a little annoyed. This was her turf. She came to their second meeting and told them in no uncertain terms, "I already got a group together. If y'all want to do this, you can join my group." It was hard to argue with a fired-up Dorothy Bolden, so they did exactly that.

Dorothy did not envision NDWU as a traditional labor union. Many unions were still segregated and treated Black members as second-class citizens—or refused to allow them to join at all. As a result, many Black workers did not have much trust in the organized labor movement. Instead, Dorothy wanted her organization to focus on changing how people looked at domestic work. In order to join the National Domestic Workers Union, a new member had to pay a fee of $1 and register to vote. Dorothy was a firm believer in the power of civic engagement, especially for Black women. The NDWU focused on training, advocacy, social services, and education. It was a sisterhood that also taught its members how to negotiate for higher wages and better treatment.

The organization developed training programs, tenant associations, and job placement initiatives specifically targeted toward lifting Black women workers out of poverty. They held "Maids' Honor Day" celebrations to publicly recognize and honor them for their labor. The group's eight original demands revolved around economics and the right to rest. They took a holistic view of what domestic workers wanted and needed. It called for minimum wages for various types of work, paid vacations, Social Security contributions from their employers, time off, sick leave, and an eight-hour workday. "I didn't organize just on money," Dorothy explained. "I organized to update the field, to make it more professional."

Within the first two years of the NDWU's existence, Atlanta's domestic workers saw their daily wages rise from less than $5 to an average $13.50 to $15.00. It wasn't quite as big of a jump as Dorothy got back at National Linen Service, but it was transformative for thousands of women. Membership grew rapidly, and they soon had 13,000 members in 10 cities. Dorothy was their champion as well as their spokesperson. She became the face of domestic work in America and traveled the country speaking about the issues they faced. She would lead the organization for the next 30 years. "I was out there for a cause and a reason," she once said. "The reason was women and the cause was there wasn't anything to live on."

Through her advocacy, Dorothy also became a political power player. During the 1970s, she was appointed to the Committee on the Status of Women's Rights and Responsibilities, where she pressed members of Congress to consider the issues poor women faced. She testified to Congress about the need for labor laws to protect domestic workers, and the necessity of enacting an hourly minimum wage and healthcare benefits. At home in Atlanta, she became an advocate for public transportation, community development, and other civic projects aimed at helping poor and working-class people. She advised Presidents Richard Nixon, Gerald Ford, and Jimmy Carter on social services and workers' rights.

Dorothy also kept the NDWU afloat as long as she could. When its federal funding dried up in the 1980s, she used her own money to keep the organization running. She finally had to close down the NDWU's office in 1994, but by then, more organizations for domestic workers had sprung up. Thanks to the work she and her coworkers began back in the 1960s, millions of domestic workers around the world now have legal protections. The National Domestic Workers Alliance (NDWA) advocates for millions of domestic workers in the U.S. Thousands of the "maids" who clean and care for households and businesses in the U.S. are now represented by strong unions like UNITE HERE (Union of Needletrades, Industrial, and Textile Employees and Hotel Employees–Restaurant Employees).

Since Dorothy's day, there have been significant legal strides for domestic workers' rights, but there is still much further to go. Domestic workers remain excluded from the 1935 National Labor Relations Act, an important law that protects workers' right to unionize. In 2010, New York passed the Domestic Workers Bill of Rights, the first statewide law to extend basic labor protections to domestic workers. Hawai'i, California, Washington, and several other states followed suit, expanding on the initial legislation with greater protections like overtime and a minimum wage. Dorothy would have loved to see the founding of International Domestic Workers Day in 2011, and to celebrate each year.

The progress Dorothy fought for is still slowly moving forward, and new generations of domestic workers have been inspired by the example she set. One thing is certain: all her hard work paid off. Dorothy herself died on July 14, 2005, at the age of 80. "I've been there for a lot of history," she once said. "I've seen history. I've made history."

Bayard Rustin
Organizing for Freedom
1912–1987

We are all one—and if we don't know it, we will learn it the hard way.

Bayard Rustin always knew that he would live an extraordinary life. He was born on March 17, 1912, into a big, complicated family. His mother, Florence, had him when she was a teenager, and his grandparents, Julia and Janifer Rustin, raised Bayard alongside their nine other children. His family history was interesting (and complicated), too. His great-grandmother Elizabeth was born free in Pennsylvania and was working as a domestic in a Quaker household when she met his great-grandfather. Janifer had been born into slavery in Maryland in 1864, and later moved North to West Chester, Pennsylvania. The couple became known as important members of the West Chester community and passed that spirit on to their children—including Bayard. He was especially close to his grandmother, who encouraged him to sing in the local church choir but also taught him about her own Quaker faith. Quakers are members of a religious movement that emphasizes building a direct relationship with their God, and spiritual equality between all people. They are also followers of pacifism, the belief that violence is unacceptable, and all problems should be solved using peaceful methods. That early education in nonviolence, conflict resolution, and individual thinking made a strong impression on Bayard, and would guide him throughout his life.

So did his grandmother's friends. Julia Rustin was an activist and took the fight against discrimination very seriously. She founded a daycare for the children of Black working mothers and was a charter member of the local branch of the National Association for the Advancement of Colored People (NAACP). She also frequently hosted legendary Black leaders like W. E. B. Du Bois, James Weldon Johnson, Mary McLeod Bethune, and Paul Robeson in her home. Even as a youngster, Bayard eagerly listened in on the grown-ups' conversations. He already knew what discrimination felt like, but those visits were how he learned about the horrors of lynchings and other racist violence against the Black community. It was a window into a much darker world outside his small hometown. It must have been frightening to hear such things, but it was important for him to understand the reality. More positively, Bayard got a firsthand look at how those Black activists and many others were trying to change things for the better.

Bayard was lucky to have been raised by a progressive, understanding family who encouraged him and all his siblings to find their own paths in life. By the time he was a teenager, Bayard knew he was attracted to boys instead of girls. When he told his grandmother that he was gay, she accepted him exactly as he was. This was a big deal in the 1920s, when gay people were often criminalized and forced to hide their true identities. But Julia Rustin said, "I suppose that's what you need to do," and loved him just the same. Knowing that his family accepted him made Bayard feel safe to explore all his interests. He excelled at school, both academically and in sports, clubs, and theater. He loved music and poetry and was an excellent public speaker. Words weren't his only talent; he was also a gifted athlete. He was especially good at football and played for a traveling team. Though he was a star on the football field, he and his other Black teammates were often discriminated against or mistreated after the games. Segregation was still enforced, and the Black teens were not always allowed to stay at the same hotels or eat at the same restaurants as their white teammates. Some all-white teams didn't even want to play against them. Bayard hated having to endure this kind of treatment. Even as a young man, he knew it was wrong. He wanted to stand up for what was right.

After graduating high school. Bayard attended two

different universities, Wilberforce and Cheyney. Neither was the right fit for him, though, so he packed up and moved to New York City. There, he took some courses at City College and taught English classes for immigrant children. His neighborhood, Harlem, was in the midst of an amazing artistic and political moment. As a former theater kid, Bayard was thrilled to be a part of it. He joined a singing group, and even performed in the choir of a Broadway play starring his old friend Paul Robeson. His horizons expanded politically, too. He joined the Young Communist League because he admired their stance on racial equality, but the association did not last long. He turned away from the organization in 1941, when it ordered its American chapters to abandon their civil rights work in favor of encouraging the U.S. to join the war and come to the Soviet Union's defense. It did not take him long to find a new political home that came with an important new mentor who would shape the next several decades of his life.

Bayard first met A. Philip Randolph during his Communist League days, but the older man was not interested in working together due to his own negative opinion of the organization. Once Bayard cut ties with them, the two men reconnected, and Randolph decided to give him a chance. While Bayard was still a young man trying to find his way in the movement, Randolph was already a legend.

His work organizing the Brotherhood of Sleeping Car Porters in 1925 cemented his legacy as a powerful labor leader. He had since become a national spokesperson for Black civil rights. In 1941, he had another big, ambitious idea—and he wanted Bayard to help!

Randolph's idea was to organize a huge march on Washington, D.C., and lead thousands of Black people to the Capitol to protest racial discrimination. They planned to call for an end to segregation in public life and in the armed forces. The U.S. had not yet entered World War II, but its defense industry was humming, providing weapons and other supplies to the Allies. Although Black workers were helping keep the economy at home running—and would later be called overseas to fight and die—they were discriminated against and treated as second-class citizens at work and in their day-to-day lives. Randolph wanted to force the government to change that. He threatened to bring 50,000 Black activists to Washington to protest. Bayard was invited to join the planning committee for the event. He was excited to see what happened, and especially admired Randolph's commitment to nonviolent direct action. But Randolph agreed to cancel the march after President Franklin D. Roosevelt issued the Fair Employment Act on June 25, 1941. The act prohibited ethnic and racial discrimination in the defense industry and federal agencies but did not desegregate the military or address the march organizers' other demands. Bayard was furious. He saw the cancellation as a betrayal of everything they had worked toward. He took things a step further by publicly criticizing Randolph for backing down. The disagreement damaged their friendship, and they did not work together for years afterward.

Bayard had plenty of other things to focus on, though. He turned his attention to the anti-war movement. As a Quaker, war was against everything he believed in. He became involved in several organizations committed to nonviolence, including the Fellowship of Reconciliation (FOR) and the Congress of Racial Equality (CORE). In 1943, he refused to register for the draft because of his pacifist beliefs. He was arrested and was sent to federal prison for three years. It was a difficult time, especially because the prison was segregated, and Bayard and the other Black prisoners were regularly mistreated. Bayard refused to let the prison break his spirit. He organized multiple protests against segregation behind bars, and jumped right back into movement work when he was finally freed in 1947.

That year, as part of a multiracial group of activists, Bayard participated in the Journey of Reconciliation, a series of civil disobedience actions. In order to test a recent Supreme Court decision barring segregated seating in interstate travel, a group of 15 men—eight white, seven

Black—traveled via bus through 15 Southern cities. It was the first of the iconic Freedom Rides. The group's white members sat at the back of the bus while Black men sat at the front, daring authorities to break the law. Twelve of the 15 were arrested. Bayard himself was sentenced to 30 days on a chain gang as punishment. Chain gangs are an awful form of punishment, where prisoners are literally chained together with heavy iron shackles. One of the police officers who arrested him got frustrated by his peaceful attitude and spat, "You're supposed to be scared when you come in here!" Rustin's answer then may as well sum up his entire lifetime of service: "I am fortified by truth, justice, and Christ.... There is no need to fear."

His legal troubles did not sway his devotion to the cause. As the years went by, Bayard became increasingly interested in global struggles. Thinking about what he'd experienced during WWII, he made a connection between the way that Black Americans were being oppressed at home with the way other people were struggling overseas. In 1942, Bayard had spent time in California helping defend the property of the more than 120,000 Japanese Americans who had been imprisoned in internment camps by the U.S. government during the war. Later, in 1948, he went to India to learn more about Gandhi's nonviolent teachings, which would come in handy when he returned to the U.S.

Bayard was arrested several times throughout his long career of organizing and protesting. While most were in service to the movement, one of those arrests, in 1953, was much more personal. It also caused problems with his colleagues in the labor and civil rights movements. It had to do with his identity. Though some progress had been made, the 1950s were still a dangerous time to be a gay person. People like Bayard were treated like criminals when their personal lives became public—and were even thrown into jail. When it happened to him, Bayard was forced to resign from his leadership position at FOR. Its director, A. J. Muste, was a former union organizer and longtime mentor, but he feared that Bayard's arrest would damage the organization's reputation. This situation would repeat itself several times throughout Rustin's life; prejudice against him for his refusal to conceal his true self gave others an excuse to sideline him, disregard his talents, or cut him out entirely.

Some of his colleagues did stand up for him, though. One of them was a young preacher named Dr. Martin Luther King Jr. He invited Bayard down to Montgomery, Alabama, to teach Black leaders about nonviolent civil disobedience. Local civil rights leaders were planning a boycott of the city's segregated bus system, and Dr. King knew that they needed Bayard's expertise. Unfortunately, Bayard did not get the chance to participate in the action.

A local reporter threatened to publish a story about his identity and past arrests, so instead Bayard was smuggled out of Alabama in the trunk of a car. He had to cheer on the Montgomery bus boycotts from the safety of his Harlem apartment. Bayard got his chance to get his hands dirty several years later, when another march was looming and some of those leaders who had once rejected him needed his help.

The 1963 March on Washington for Jobs and Freedom is regarded as one of the most impactful political demonstrations in U.S. history—and one of its chief organizers was a gay Black man. During the planning stages for the march, Bayard was brought in by the "Big Six" leaders. They were: his old friend, A. Philip Randolph; John Lewis, chairman of the Student Nonviolent Coordinating Committee (SNCC); CORE cofounder James Farmer; NAACP executive secretary Roy Wilkins; Whitney Young, the executive director of the National Urban League; and Southern Christian Leadership Conference (SCLC) chairman Dr. King. They knew that Rustin had more direct organizing experience and understanding of nonviolent tactics than the rest of them put together. As John Lewis later recalled, "This was going to be a massively complex undertaking, and there was no one more able to pull it together than Bayard Rustin." Bayard got to work, drawing up an agenda and orchestrating every tiny detail of the event. That day, 250,000 people would peacefully assemble on the National Mall and cry out for freedom.

As author William P. Jones explained in his book *The March on Washington: Jobs, Freedom, and the Forgotten History of Civil Rights*, Rustin's main goal for the march was rooted in economics. He wanted to draw attention to "the economic subordination of the Negro," create "more jobs for all Americans," and advance a "broad and fundamental program for economic justice." He had seven weeks to plan it, and its execution was almost perfect. The only sour note was the exclusion of women like Rosa Parks and Ella Baker, pivotal activists and organizers, who were denied the spotlight by their male counterparts. They should have been given their moment in the sun alongside their brothers, and Bayard should have recognized how important it was to include everyone.

For all his efforts, Bayard Rustin was never publicly named march director. Instead, he was called Randolph's deputy. But when it became clear that it had been a massive success, he was hailed as a hero. Several prestigious civil rights organizations offered to hire him, but as usual, he decided to go his own way. In 1965, he founded the A. Philip Randolph Institute, an organization with a focus on racial equality and economic justice. The APRI's mission was to strengthen the place of Black workers in the labor movement. He also began to talk more about his ideas on Black economic empowerment. Bayard believed that unions offered the best means for ending discrimination, saying that the economic boost that comes from union membership would uplift the most vulnerable Black folks and thus, the entire community. It was an echo of what people like Rosina Tucker had said decades earlier.

However, Bayard's politics began to shift even further into an unexpected direction. His interest in racial justice activism faded, and he criticized Black political thinkers who he saw as too radical. He began to advocate working within the system, instead of trying to build a new one. This development surprised some of his old friends, who had spent decades fighting alongside him specifically for racial justice. It also made him enemies within the growing Black power movement and alienated some of his comrades in the civil rights struggle. Bayard's political views became more and more conservative, and even his lifelong anti-war stance seemed to shift when the U.S. launched its war on Vietnam. His deeply anti-communist stance also led him to participate in numerous political committees and actions that shocked his socialist friends in the labor movement. His politics, like his personal life, were complicated, and he refused to apologize for either.

Throughout it all, Bayard continued throwing himself into the causes he felt were most essential. He traveled the globe advocating against human rights abuses in other countries and did the same in the American South. In 1968, for example, he heard about a group of sanitation workers in Memphis, Tennessee, who'd just gone on strike to protest horrible working conditions and racial discrimination on the job. An old friend of his was scheduled to speak in support of their action. Bayard packed his bags and hit the road.

The Memphis Sanitation Strike had begun on February 12, 1968. Nearly 1,000 members of the American Federation of State, County and Municipal Employees (AFSCME) Local 1733 went on strike after two of their fellow sanitation workers, Echol Cole and Robert Walker, were crushed by a garbage compactor. Their deaths were a horrific symbol of how little the labor and lives of these Black workers were valued by the city. Their names became a rallying cry. The workers wanted recognition of their union and an end to racial discrimination in the Memphis Public Works Department. As the strike went on, the workers refused to complete their usual trash pickups. Tons of stinking garbage piled up in the street as strikers rallied under the slogan "I Am a Man!" and held firm in the face of police brutality. Steelworkers Local URW 186, which boasted the largest Black membership in Memphis, stepped up to offer their support. Sadly, the city's other predominantly white unions stayed away from the Black sanitation workers' public struggle. News of the strike reached Bayard and other civil rights leaders, including his old friend Dr. King. "If I were the mayor of this city, I would be ashamed," Bayard told a crowd of strikers on March 14, 1968. "I wouldn't want these men to not be able to feed their families on the lousy pittance they are paid."

Dr. King visited Memphis several times throughout the course of the strike, marching alongside the workers and their supporters. While Bayard's connections with labor were more prominent, Dr. King was a union man as well. He spoke often about the dignity of labor and the importance of unions to protect workers' rights. When he arrived in Memphis on April 3, he gave one of the most impactful speeches of his life. It was a real showstopper. In the "I've Been to the Mountaintop" sermon, Dr. King spoke of the workers' struggle and the dire need to stand with them as they struggled. He challenged the crowd to answer the question, "If I do not stop to help the sanitation workers, what will happen to them?" Unfortunately, the great man would not live to find out. The next day, Dr. King was dead, assassinated on his hotel balcony. Bayard was asked to give interviews after the assassination and was unable to keep the tears from streaming down his face. "It is up to us," he said then, "the living, the Black and white, to realize Dr. King's dream."

After all those years of hardship, hard work, and heartbreak, Bayard spent the rest of his life doing exactly what he'd planned on all those years ago: fighting for what he thought was right. Bayard himself lived to a ripe old age. He died in 1987 at the age of 75, with his longtime partner, Walter Naegle, at his side. Since then, he's been honored in countless ways, from having schools named after him to being awarded the Presidential Medal of Freedom. In 2020, California governor Gavin Newsom issued a pardon for Bayard's 1953 arrest, finally wiping clean a record that should never have been created in the first place.

Nagi Daifullah
The Dreamer Turned Martyr
1949-1973

Dearest father, you will be amazed at this which I am writing to you . . .

Nagi Daifullah did not set out to change the world. When he was a little boy growing up in the North Yemen village of Kahlan, he dreamed of moving to America to study medicine. He wanted to help people—that was why he wanted to become a doctor. But once he actually made it to the United States, the plan changed. Instead of going to medical school, Nagi became involved with a movement that would make him a legend—and a martyr.

Details about his early years are hard to find, but we know Nagi was born in Yemen in 1949. When he was ten, his parents sent him to a British school in South Yemen. That was where he first developed his political consciousness. He learned about imperialism from British teachers whose homeland had colonized his own; he must have been an awfully good student, for he was later arrested for tearing a British flag off the wall at school. As Neama

Alamri, PhD, found in her research into his life, by the time he went to university in the city of Ta'izz, he was a full-fledged anti-imperialist. It was the right time and place to be one. After a century of colonial rule, Nagi wasn't the only young Yemeni who was fed up with the British. It was the 1960s, and Yemen was in the midst of a political upheaval. In 1967, Marxist activists in South Yemen forced the British to hand over control of the country, establishing the People's Democratic Republic of Yemen. In 1968, North Yemenis rebelled against the British monarchy and became the Republic of Yemen. Conflicts between the two new states erupted, and the ensuing economic crisis led to a large wave of immigration. Among them was 19-year-old Nagi, who joined thousands of other Yemeni men who hoped to find work in the United States. He still wanted to become a doctor but soon found that his talents were needed elsewhere.

Most of the new Yemeni immigrants ended up in Detroit auto factories, but about 5,000 made their way to California. There, they joined Mexican and Filipino agricultural workers in the lush fields of the San Joaquin Valley. The Yemenis were initially welcomed by employers who assumed the Arab workers would be "docile" and easy to boss around. (It certainly wouldn't be the first time bosses' own prejudices ended up working against them!) Like the Filipinos they worked alongside, many of the

Yemeni workers came armed with a politically radical outlook and a fearless hunger to organize. Nagi may have seemed like a shy, unassuming young man upon a first glance, but like his coworkers, he had the heart of a lion. He was determined to make a decent living so he could help his family back home. "Dearest father, I arrived in America to continue my studies as I had dreamed," he wrote in a letter. "But because living conditions are hard and because study in America is very difficult, I feel rather that I owe you some financial assistance."

As soon as he arrived in California, Nagi began learning English and Spanish. He was a quick learner, and soon found a job as a translator for the United Farm Workers. The union was in the middle of organizing farmworkers across the state, and they needed to be able to connect with workers in multiple languages. Nagi played a crucial role in fostering that understanding and solidarity through his interactions with Mexican, Filipino, and Yemeni workers. He also brought his own political viewpoints and passion to the job. "He was very courageous, encouraging us and telling us, 'This is democracy, and if you want your rights, this is how you do it,'" said Ahmed Yahya Mushreh, a former grape picker and UFW member who marched alongside Nagi, and now works as a janitor with SEIU Local 87. "You fight for your rights. This is the United States."

UFW union leaders noticed his skills in bridging the

gaps between communities and cultures as well as his gift with languages. Nagi was soon hired as a full-time organizer. "I am now working in agriculture with our Arab and Spanish and Indian and Filipino brethren," he wrote in a letter to his father. "Working in the grape fields is tougher than coal-mining, because the work is for longer hours, and the workers are exposed to maltreatment by the greedy capitalist landowners. And agricultural workers here have no collective representation to protect them and to undertake demands for their rights and sufficient assurances for them, like those for the workers in factories and other sectors."

Nagi had come along at just the right time, too, because when 1973 rolled around, the UFW were facing another momentous labor action. It would be known as the Salad Bowl Strike and would have an unimaginable impact on Nagi's life.

Instead of pitting workers against their bosses, this conflict was a turf war between rival unions. The UFW faced off against the Teamsters, who had made a special deal with the growers following their own strike in 1970. In exchange for giving them the exclusive right to organize workers in their fields, the Teamsters cut "sweetheart deals" with growers to keep the UFW out. These deals hurt workers by cutting pay and reducing their rights. They also undercut the UFW's own organizing. The farmworkers tried to make a more reasonable agreement with the Teamsters, but negotiations fell through. What began as a spat over union territory turned into a series of bitter strikes, mass pickets, boycotts, and secondary boycotts that would escalate into the largest farmworker strike in U.S. history. That year, between 5,000 and 7,000 Yemeni, Mexican, and Filipino farmworkers walked out of the fields and onto the picket line.

It quickly turned ugly. The local police reacted violently to the strikers, and arrested thousands of farmworkers. They were also documented beating and macing hundreds of them and their supporters—including priests and nuns. As tensions between the strikers, the UFW, the Teamsters, and the police increased, Daifullah took on a greater role as a strike captain. The UFW's César Chávez praised his dedication, saying, "He [...] gave himself fully to the grape strike and farmworker justice." The young organizer's courage took him out onto the front lines, but also painted a target on his back.

On August 15, 1973, Nagi was standing outside the Smokehouse Café in Lamont, California, chatting with a group of farmworkers when three Kern County sheriffs pulled up and started harassing them. They tried to arrest UFW picket captain Frank Quintana. Nagi and the other workers began to argue with them, asking them to let him go. The cops then turned their attention on Nagi.

He didn't want to risk getting in trouble himself, so he decided to leave. They chased after him, and as he ran, Deputy Gilbert Cooper smashed his heavy flashlight into the back of Nagi's head and severed his spinal cord. The two other deputies then dragged Nagi's limp body across the pavement by his feet. They bumped his head along the ground, leaving a smear of blood on the concrete. Then they threw his mangled body in the gutter and arrested three of the workers he'd been trying to protect. It was a horrific day.

The shocking brutality of the attack hit the farmworker community hard. That night, thousands of supporters held a vigil outside the hospital where he lay, praying for him to heal. Tragically, Nagi did not survive his injuries. He died at the age of 24.

Nagi's adopted community showed up for him until the end. Seven thousand people accompanied his casket on a funeral parade that stretched for 11 miles. "That entire march, not a word was spoken, not one word," UFW organizer Roy Cordova, who was present that day, remembered. "People were not talking to each other. They weren't whispering. All you could hear was a shuffle of the feet on the pavement. It was a very solemn tribute to Nagi." UFW leader César Chávez spoke at the funeral, and later wrote to his father in Yemen, "So long as farmworkers struggle to be free, Nagi's memory will burn bright in their hearts." His body was sent home to Yemen for a much-deserved rest. The UFW sent Nagi's father a monthly support check for the rest of his life. Meanwhile, the police officer who killed him was never charged with a crime.

Nagi's murder inspired the strikers to fight even harder in his memory. A new group of Arab farmworkers even joined the strike after hearing the news of his death. His sacrifice also inspired the union to intensify its fight for farmworkers' rights. There was still no statewide law in California allowing farmworkers the legal right to organize (nor was there a federal version). In 1974, the UFW began lobbying California governor Jerry Brown to reform the state's labor laws to fix this problem. Union leaders and farmworkers went on a 110-mile march from San Francisco to Modesto to draw attention to their demand. Sixty-eight days later, California passed the 1975 California Agricultural Labor Relations Act, which established collective bargaining rights for farmworkers. It was the first law of its kind in the country. Its passage was a massive victory for the UFW, and for all of California's farmworkers.

They did not forget the sacrifice that got them to that point, either. When they gathered later that year to vote in the first legal union elections, there were many Yemenis from the San Joaquin Valley among them. They cast their votes in honor of Nagi Daifullah.

Judy Heumann
The Unstoppable Activist
1947–2023

We stood for inclusiveness and community, for our love of equity and justice—and we won.

It was the first day of kindergarten, and Judy was so excited that she could barely sit still. It seemed as though she'd been waiting her whole life for this day. She had just turned five years old and she was dying to meet girls and boys her own age. It was a big day for everyone in her house, too. Her mother, Ilse, had even gotten her a pretty new dress for the occasion. When it came time to leave, Judy sat up in her wheelchair and rolled as fast as she could go. When they arrived at her new school, her mother carried her the rest of the way up the steps. Everything was going perfectly—until the principal appeared. He told her mother that Judy was not allowed inside. She and her daughter were both shocked. Surely he was joking? But there was no trace of a smile on his stern face. The principal insisted that Judy's wheelchair was a fire hazard. She would be a danger to the other children if an emergency happened. Now Ilse was angry, but Judy was still confused. She couldn't understand what was wrong with her or her wheelchair. Other kids her age were running up the steps and right through the doors for class. Why couldn't she go to school, too?

Judy and her mother were turned away that day, but neither of them was ready to admit defeat. Ilse was tough as nails. She had to be. Her family had escaped Germany in 1935 when the Nazis came to power and started targeting Jewish people like them. The same thing had happened to Judy's father, Werner. They had found one another and started a new life together in the U.S. Now he ran a butcher shop in their Brooklyn neighborhood. Her parents knew what it felt like to be singled out for who they were, but Judy was only a little girl. Until that day, she hadn't realized she was any different from any of her friends. Her chair was just part of who she was, like her brown eyes or big smile. How could someone see it and think of it as a problem—or worse, a threat?

The first few years of Judy Heumann's life had been pretty eventful, it was true. She was born in Philadelphia on December 18, 1947, but grew up in Brooklyn, New York. When she was 18 months old, she came down with polio. The disease had swept through the country in 1949, sickening thousands of children. Terrified parents watched their kids closely for any signs of polio's telltale fatigue and muscle weakness. Many of the children who survived lost the use of their limbs. Judy was one of them. She was quadriplegic—she no longer had the ability to move her legs. That was why she used a wheelchair to get around. It had been a part of her life for as long as she could remember.

Her mother tried and tried, but no schools would accept her daughter. There were very few good options for a child like Judy. The city gave in and sent a tutor to Judy's house for a few hours each day, but it was nowhere near enough. She had to do most of her learning on her own. As a bright and inquisitive kid, she was hungry for knowledge. Judy read books, took piano lessons, and went to Hebrew classes to learn about her family's Jewish culture. All the while, her mother kept petitioning the city to properly educate her gifted daughter. It took years of persistence, but Judy was finally accepted into a special program for disabled students. She had her very first day of school when she was nine years old, four years after the other kids her age had started their first day of school. It was still school, though, and Judy adapted quickly to her new routine.

It soon became clear that the program wasn't a great fit for her, either. She made friends with the other disabled students, but her class was a jumble of different age groups. Some of them were older than her, and others were younger. They all had different levels of education yet were put into the same class and given the same work. They were also separated from the rest of the school and never had any opportunities to mingle or make new friends. It felt like they were being hidden away. Their classes were even held in the school's basement. Judy did not think anything about it was fair (she was right—it was in fact illegal) but she decided to make the best of it and learn everything she could.

Now that Judy was finally in school, she was determined to stay there. She didn't realize that the clock started ticking as soon as she stepped foot in that basement. Ilse discovered that the city had a rule that disabled children had to return home once they reached high school age. She and Judy were exasperated—they had already fought so hard to get her into classes, and now she only had a few years before she'd be kicked out again? Clearly the rules had to be changed. Ilse began meeting with other parents of disabled youth to strategize. Their group successfully pressured the school board into changing the rule, and Judy started high school in 1961. She was an excellent student (especially now that she could finally study in peace!).

After that, she went to college at Long Island University. Some of her classmates in the basement school had struggled to speak, and the memory of their frustration and sadness at being isolated inspired her to study speech therapy. She decided that she would become a teacher.

During her time at Long Island University, she also became politically active. Although she was able to attend classes without being hassled, it was still difficult for her to physically get into the school buildings. She organized protests with other students calling on the university to add wheelchair ramps, and to allow disabled students to live in the dorms alongside their classmates. Judy was getting pretty tired of seeing disabled people denied the opportunity to live a normal life.

It had taken Judy so much extra effort to get an education that once she received her diploma, she could hardly wait to start using it. In 1970, she passed almost all her teaching exams with flying colors. The last one she took had nothing to do with her skills as an educator. It was a physical examination, and she failed. As a result, the school board refused to approve her teaching license. To Judy's horror, they called her wheelchair a fire hazard—again. She must have been taken right back to that moment when she was five and a strange man was telling her that her very presence was a problem. Now that she was an adult, she was not going to let them get away with it again. Judy argued to the board that she could move more quickly in her motorized wheelchair than any other teacher could walking. And if the school added a ramp and allowed her to use a classroom on the ground floor, she would easily be able to escort students out during an emergency. She wasn't a danger, she was an asset. But they still wouldn't let her teach.

Unfortunately for them, Judy's mother had raised her to be a fighter. The young teacher decided to go above the board's heads to argue her case. She sued the Board of Education for discrimination—and won. She got her teaching license a few months later. Judy became the first wheelchair user to teach in the New York public school system and taught at an elementary school for three years. Judy had also become something of a celebrity after the newspapers reported on her story. Other disabled people took her story to heart. Many of them knew exactly how she had felt and sent her letters sharing their own issues and experiences. The outpouring of support made Judy realize that she was not alone. There were lots of other disabled people out there just like her who wanted to fight for equal treatment and opportunities

In 1970, she and a few friends started Disabled in Action (DIA), an activist group focused on disabled people's civil rights. They were inspired by the protest movements for Black civil rights and women's rights, and against the Vietnam War. There were obvious parallels between these movements and the disabled activists' own experiences. In the eyes of the government, they didn't count as full citizens. DIA got their chance to act two years later when President Nixon vetoed the

Rehabilitation Act of 1972. This law would have prohibited discrimination on the basis of disability in programs conducted and funded by the federal government. Yet Nixon shot it down. It was a huge disappointment.

Judy and DIA wanted to call attention to the issue, and they weren't interested in being polite about it. They "really felt that we had to take what we considered the anger and oppression that we were experiencing as disabled people and not sit around and complain about it," she later explained. So on November 3, 1972, she and 30 other activists rolled their wheelchairs into the middle of New York City's busy Madison Avenue. They blocked rush hour traffic, shutting down the whole street for almost an hour. It was loud, visible, and disruptive—exactly what they'd wanted. After that, DIA continued to hold rallies and protests for disabled people's rights. "If you believe in something, do whatever you have to do to get your point across," Judy later wrote in her 2020 memoir. She didn't know it then, but she and her friends would change the world by spending the next few years doing exactly that.

The Rehabilitation Act was finally passed in 1973. Section 504 of the law was especially important. It was the first federal civil rights protection for disabled people. It was modeled on the Civil Rights Act and prevented federal employers from discriminating against disabled workers. Basically, it would have been illegal for any government-funded company to refuse to hire a disabled person on the basis of their disability. It was extremely difficult at that time for many disabled people to find jobs because of this exact kind of discrimination. The community was very hopeful that the law would change that. However, the government dragged its feet on implementing the necessary regulations that would have made Section 504 enforceable. Disabled activists began calling on Nixon's Health, Education, and Welfare secretary, Joseph A. Califano Jr., to hurry up. As their letters and phone calls were ignored, months turned into years.

Meanwhile, in 1975, Judy moved to California. She had been invited by disability rights leader Ed Roberts to come work at the Center for Independent Living. The independent living movement advocated for disabled people's ability to participate in society and make decisions about their own lives. This was obviously right up Judy's alley. It was exactly what she had been fighting for since she was a little girl. Disabled people are the experts on their own needs, and centers like the one where Judy worked in Berkeley provided resources to the disabled community. It was the perfect place for her to channel her activist energy into community support. Judy wasn't finished with school, either. She enrolled at the University of California, Berkeley and graduated with a master's degree in public health.

While Judy was busy with her new job and new

classes, the Rehabilitation Act had continued to sit in limbo. By now, it had been several years since the law was passed, yet the government had still not taken any action to put it into practice. Section 504 was nothing but some words on a fancy piece of paper. Judy turned her attention to the struggle to force them to act. She and her friends decided they needed to turn up the heat. Phone calls and letters had not worked. For years, disabled activists had been asking nicely to have their concerns addressed. Once again, it was time to stop playing nice. Luckily, Judy had some experience in that area. On April 5, 1977, she and her fellow activists took their demands straight to the Department of Health, Education, and Welfare agency's doorstep.

What happened next was organized by disabled activist Kitty Cone, a wheelchair user with a long history of involvement in various social justice movements. Judy led the on-the-ground operations. They and 100 other disabled protesters, interpreters, and personal care aides occupied the H.E.W.'s fourth-floor offices in the San Francisco Federal Building for 26 days straight. It became known as the 504 Sit-In, because that section of the law was their primary focus. Shorter sit-ins also took place at the agency's offices in Atlanta, Boston, Chicago, Denver, Los Angeles, Philadelphia, and Seattle. "It began with a rally outside the federal building, then we marched inside where between 1 and 200 people would remain until the end," Kitty remembered. "We all felt that we were acting on behalf of hundreds of thousands of people who were not able to participate."

Government officials responded to their protest by shutting off the building's water, trying to block food and medication deliveries, and cutting off the phone lines. The activists inside cared for one another as conditions deteriorated. Local churches, community groups, Vietnam veterans, and political organizations also came to the protestors' aid. Activist Brad Lomax, who had multiple sclerosis and was a wheelchair user, and his aide, Chuck Jackson, were both members of the Black Panther Party. During the 504 Sit-In, he and Jackson asked their local Black Panther Party for help. They immediately stepped in to provide daily hot meals and other supplies to the demonstrators. Without those supplies, fellow activist Corbett O'Toole later wrote, "the sit-in would have collapsed."

Two weeks into the sit-in, a delegation of activists (including Brad, Judy, and Kitty) went to Washington, D.C., to meet with senators Alan Cranston and Harrison Williams. The Black Panthers paid for their plane tickets. Organized labor also contributed support once they got to D.C. The International Association of Machinists (IAM) rented a U-Haul truck with a lift on the back to transport the group's wheelchair users around the city. As

Kitty remembered, the union went above and beyond to support the disabled activists. "[The IAM] allowed us to use their union headquarters to organize demonstrations, so we had access to telephone lines, copy machines, and other things necessary for organizing," she recalled.

A special congressional hearing was convened. The activists testified, one by one, about what Section 504 meant for them and their community. "We want the law enforced," Judy testified. "We will accept no more discussion of segregation." Frank Bowe, a Deaf man who was the director of American Coalition of Citizens with Disabilities, spoke last. His remarks left the crowd in tears as he said, "Senator, we are not even second-class citizens, we are third-class citizens."

The sit-in, the media coverage, the community support, and the strength and determination of the activists themselves all made their mark. Public support was behind the activists' demand. On April 28, 1977, Califano quietly signed the regulations. Judy and her friends declared victory. They'd done it! They had won! The occupation was over. It had become the longest peaceful occupation of a federal building in U.S. history. As the activists finally walked and wheeled out of the San Francisco Federal Building two days later, they sang "We Shall Overcome" at the top of their voices. "The sit-in was a truly transforming experience, the likes of which most of us had never seen before or ever saw again," Kitty wrote on its 20th anniversary. "For the first time, many of us felt proud of who we were. And we understood that our isolation and segregation stemmed from societal policy, not from some personal defects on our part, and our experiences with segregation and discrimination were not just our own personal problems."

Section 504 was not a perfect law. It had limits. For one, it only applied to federally funded projects. Private employers could still do whatever they wanted—for a few more years. Section 504's greatest impact was that it laid the groundwork for the 1990 Americans with Disabilities Act. That law expanded its protections to include workers in private institutions and workplaces. The government didn't put the law into place on its own, though. It took more organizing efforts and another round of protests from a new generation of activists to get it done. This time they were led by a group called ADAPT, then known as Americans Disabled for Accessible Public Transit. On March 13, 1990, over 1,000 people marched from the White House to the Capitol to demand the ADA's passage. When they reached the building, 60 disabled protestors got out of their wheelchairs and dropped their mobility aids. As news cameras captured their every move, they slowly crawled up the Capitol steps on their hands and knees. The crawl was led by an 8-year-old girl with cerebral palsy named Jennifer Keelan. Jennifer attended her first disability rights protest when she was only six years old. Just like Judy, she had been fighting against discrimination for her entire young life. "I wanted to make sure that not only my generation of kids with disabilities would be represented, but future generations of kids with disabilities as well," she explained in a 2020 interview.

They won their battle, too. The ADA marked another critical moment for the disability rights movement. It was a victory for the hundreds of disabled activists who'd fought for it, and for every disabled person's right to be treated as equal citizens under the law. They were no longer "third-class citizens." It took multiple generations of disabled activists to get there. It's beautiful to think that one of the first big chapters in the modern disability rights movement began with a disabled girl in Brooklyn who just wanted to go to school with her friends. The next chapter was led by another little disabled girl who wanted to make sure her own generation's voices would be heard. "We looked beyond how we each spoke and moved, how we thought and how we looked," Judy wrote in her memoir as she looked back on that era of struggle. "We stood for inclusiveness and community, for our love of equity and justice—and we won."

Those protests were only the beginning of Judy's long career as a disability rights activist. She earned the title

"The Mother of the Disability Rights Movement" for all her work. Policy and legislation became her big focus. She helped develop other important legislation, including the Individuals with Disabilities Education Act and the U.N. Convention on the Rights of Persons with Disabilities. She even found time to fall in love with Jorge Pineda, another disabled activist and wheelchair user. They married in 1991.

Judy later went back to Washington D.C.—and this time, it wasn't for a protest. In 1993, President Bill Clinton appointed her the assistant secretary of the Office of Special Education and Rehabilitative Services. From 1993 to 2001, Judy was in charge of all the nation's federal education programs for disabled students. She made sure none of them were hidden away in a gloomy basement like she had been. Those memories of exclusion had never left her, and she never wanted another child to feel that way. The world had changed since 1952, but Judy knew there was still much work to be done. She also knew that she wanted to be one of the people doing it.

Judy eventually took her message of disability rights global. She traveled the world meeting with disabled activists and stayed busy in Washington, D.C. She advised organizations like the World Bank, the Ford Foundation and Human Rights Watch. During the Obama administration, she was appointed the first Special Advisor for International Disability Rights in the U.S. Department of

State, where she served from 2010 until 2017. Her efforts made an impact, and that impact won her much-deserved honors and acclaim. Judy was featured in multiple documentaries and received countless awards for her advocacy work. The girl who'd had to fight so hard to go to school was even awarded honorary doctorate degrees from New York University, University of Pittsburgh, Middlebury College, and Smith College.

Judy Heumann died in 2023 at the age of 75. Her loss left a huge hole in the disability rights community, but the work she did and the legacy she left behind has inspired new generations of disabled activists to continue the fight. "People need to dream, they need to believe they can dream, and they need to have the right to pursue and attain those dreams," she once said. "We have to work for them, but we shouldn't have to do more work just because we have disabilities."

Silme Domingo and Gene Viernes
The Rank-and-File Reformers
1951/1952–1981

Silme and Gene were just ordinary people who became part of an extraordinary movement.... —Cindy Domingo, sister of Silme

Silme and Gene were two peas in a pod. Everyone knew that wherever Gene was, Silme wasn't far behind, and vice versa. They were best friends, coworkers, and proud troublemakers. While one wore flashy bell-bottoms and platform shoes, the other rocked a beat-up jean jacket, but they both saw the world the same way. Their job had brought them together, but their bond went deeper than union meetings and fish guts. The two of them had very different personalities and had led very different lives before their paths crossed, but once together, they were unstoppable.

Silme Domingo was born in Killeen, Texas, in 1952. When Silme was eight years old, his father, Nemesio, decided to pack up and move them all to Seattle, Washington. Nemesio worked in the Alaskan fish canneries where many other Filipino immigrant workers spent their summers. It was a physically demanding, often dangerous job, but the pay was decent. When he was 17, Silme eventually joined him in the cannery. There, the teen worked as a "slimer," a cannery worker who cleans fish by hand using a very sharp knife. The cannery was kept chilly to prevent the fish from spoiling, and their guts splattered everywhere. The shivering workers did their best to stay warm, but each day was a losing battle against the cold.

There were also other, bigger issues with the work environment. The Filipino workers and the Native Alaskan workers at the cannery were segregated from the white employees. Their cafeterias served lower quality food, and they were made to sleep in cold, dirty bunkhouses. Meanwhile, the white workers enjoyed much better food (and cleaner accommodations). The blatant discrimination stuck in Silme's craw. His father cautioned him to swallow his pride and worry about his paycheck, but Silme wasn't the kind of person who could let it slide. Every time he clocked in for a shift, he quietly fumed.

Meanwhile, Gene Viernes was dealing with nearly identical working conditions in another cannery in Ketchikan, Alaska. He got his start on the slime line even earlier than Silme. They were both Alaskeros, which was a nickname for the many Filipino and Filipino American workers who traveled to Alaska seasonally for work. It was one heck of a long commute, but the job paid well and there were few other opportunities open to them. This seasonal loop took them from California's fields to Washington's fruit orchards to Alaskan canneries, and back again. "When the spring field work comes to a grinding halt, many Filipino workers migrate north to find the one job available to them: sliming fish in the chilly fish houses of Alaska," Gene wrote later. "They have tried but cannot find work elsewhere, lack necessary skills, schooling, or resources, and are prevented from gaining jobs."

Gene's father got him a job at a cannery when he was only 15. The legal age to work was 16, but he solved that problem by bribing union officials to allow the young teenager to work anyway. Gene had grown up on a farm in Washington State's lush Yakima Valley, so he had a hard time adjusting to the brutal Alaskan weather and horrible working conditions. He was far more used to sunshine and fresh fruit, and the stench of the slime line was a rude awakening. So was the racism and discrimination he and his coworkers experienced on the job. He hated it just as much as Silme did. After crossing paths in the canneries one summer, the two became fast friends. It turned out that they had a lot in common.

Both Gene and Silme attended college and worked at the canneries during their summer breaks. Gene was a history major at Central Washington State College. He'd become fascinated with the history of the salmon canning industry and wrote about his research for a local union newspaper. Silme was a member of the Asian Student Coalition at his school, the University of Washington. The group organized around immigrant services and low-cost housing and monitored political conflicts happening in the Philippines. Dictator Ferdinand E. Marcos placed the country under martial law in 1972, ruling the island with an iron fist and targeting any dissenters. Many Filipinos opposed his harsh policies, but it was risky to speak publicly against him—his spies were always listening. However, Silme was all the way over in the U.S. He felt it was his duty to speak out when others wouldn't. Silme helped found the Union of Democratic Filipinos (KDP) and led protests against the Marcos regime. His time as a student activist would have an unexpected impact on his seasonal career in the canneries—and on his and Gene's futures.

As time went on, both Gene and Silme became more vocal at work. They'd held their tongues for years and could no longer stand it. They started talking to their coworkers about the unfair conditions that the Filipino and Native Alaskan workers were forced to endure. One of the few upsides of this seasonal work system was that the workers also carried their shared grievances and union sympathies with them. When union organizers showed up to talk with the cannery workers, they were often welcomed with open arms by slimers fed up with the racism, discrimination, and brutal working conditions. Gene and Silme worked at a unionized cannery thanks to decades of effort by Filipino and Native Alaskan labor organizers and rank-and-file workers.

In 1971, Silme and his brothers who worked alongside him at the cannery all received letters from their employers at the New England Fish Company (NEFCO). To their surprise, they were informed that they would not be welcomed back that summer. Not only that, they'd also all been blacklisted—added to a list of troublesome workers that the company refused to hire back. That was the last straw. Their firing kicked off a flurry of legal action. Silme, his brothers, and about three dozen other Filipino, Native Alaskan, Asian, and Latino workers filed a huge class action suit against NEFCO for discrimination. It was not a quick fix; far from it. The lawsuit was broken up into three separate cases and spent years in the court system; the last one was not resolved until 1991.

In 1973, as Silme's case made its way through the courts, Gene was informed that he'd been blacklisted, too. He joined the lawsuit, and he and Silme formed the Alaskan Cannery Workers Association (ACWA) to handle the legal dealings. Unfortunately, they did not have the support of the union that represented them and their coworkers, International Longshore and Warehouse Union (ILWU) Local 37. The union's president considered the ACWA to be a rival labor group and refused to recognize their efforts. Neither did his successor, Tony

Baruso. He was no fan of Silme and Gene's and didn't trust the progressive-minded duo.

As their lawsuits dragged on, Silme and Gene turned their attention to the union itself. It had stung when the union refused to help them and their coworkers fight discrimination in the courts. It seemed as though their local had turned a blind eye to lots of other issues, too. Local 37 was rotten with the same kind of inequality that they'd been fighting against in the canneries, as well as problems with corruption and mismanagement. The union's leadership had turned it into more of a club for their friends than a real workers' rights organization. Looking at how it was all laid out, the two young men resolved to reform the organization themselves. They wanted union democracy: to give the workers a proper say in how the union was run, instead of allowing their leaders to call all the shots. In 1977, Silme and Gene founded a Rank-and-File Committee devoted to fighting the corruption inside the union. One of Local 37's major issues at that time was favoritism. The union's dispatch system, which determined which workers would be sent out to work assignments, was supposed to operate around seniority. Instead, it was controlled by certain dispatchers and foremen. They gave the best gigs to their gambling buddies and those who could afford a bribe.

In addition, the union had a cozy relationship with

local organized crime. This led to even more dangerous complications. Some of the union leaders' "gambling buddies" were actually Tulisan gang members. They had paid their way into the canneries, where they ran gambling operations. The Rank-and-File Committee knew that cleaning up the union would be an almost insurmountable challenge, but they put their heads down and continued quietly organizing. It took them several years to build up a majority, but in 1980, when the union held its leadership elections, Silme was voted in as secretary-treasurer and Gene as a dispatcher. It was a major victory for the reformers. Unfortunately, the union's crooked leader, Tony Baruso, remained in power as president. He was not happy with how the election had gone, and neither were the gang members he was secretly aligned with.

Outside of their union activities, Gene and Silme were also deeply involved in the Filipino activist community in their adopted hometown of Seattle. They worked to build solidarity across the Filipino diaspora, and to inspire their local community to speak out against the atrocities happening back in the Philippines. In 1981, Gene took a trip to the Philippines to visit his family. He told everyone he was going on vacation, but had made some secret plans of his own. Once he arrived, he met with anti-Marcos union leaders and learned about the struggles workers faced under the Marcos regime. Things were dicey at his union in Seattle, but the Philippines was a whole other world. Some of the labor activists he met had been arrested for sedition; other union leaders had been assassinated by the regime; their unions were outlawed. The meeting shook Gene to his core. He knew he had to find a way to help, or at least draw attention to their situation. He got a chance later that year, when he and Silme attended an ILWU union convention. They stood up and asked the delegates to send an ILWU committee to investigate the conditions of workers in the Philippines. Their own union president, Baruso, was absolutely furious when he heard about what they had done. He was a staunch Marcos supporter and had friends in the regime's government.

Their request for an investigation was approved. They should have been celebrating, but those close to them say that the convention was the moment when Silme and Gene knew that their futures were in jeopardy. Silme's partner, Terri Mast, was a Rank-and-File Committee member and Filipino activist. The two of them were raising their two young daughters together. She knew that Marcos supporters would see the ILWU resolution as "a direct threat" to the Marcos regime. The regime could not afford the economic impact of any potential strikes—and would definitely not appreciate seeing their own labor movement getting a boost from an American union. Though all they'd wanted to do was help Filipino workers,

Gene and Silme realized that they were playing with fire. Soon, they both began to see unfamiliar cars following them and their family members around. Strangers glared out at them from the windows. It was nerve-racking. The Marcos regime was known to be merciless toward dissenters, even ones living overseas. Gene and Silme became anxious about their safety and that of their loved ones. Silme even went to the Local 37 board with a very specific request: he wanted to buy life insurance.

His instincts were correct. On June 1, 1981, two armed Tulisan gang members broke into the ILWU union office in Seattle looking for Gene and Silme. Upon finding the men, they pulled out their guns and shot them both. Gene died immediately. Silme, shot four times in the stomach, made it outside. As bystanders crowded around him, he gasped out the names of the men who'd shot them. He died the next day. Pompeyo Benito Guloy and Jimmy Bulosan Ramil, Local 37 members and Tulisan enforcers, were eventually arrested for their murder and sentenced to life in prison. So was gang leader Tony Dictado, who had ordered the murder and driven the getaway car. The police also questioned Baruso, but let him go.

The loss of Gene and Silme was devastating. The two young men were only 29 when they were gunned down. To honor their sacrifices, their surviving family members and labor friends continued the work they'd begun together.

Terri Mast and Silme's sister, Cindy Domingo, worked alongside dozens of activists to create the Committee for Justice for Domingo and Viernes. They refused to give up on holding their loved ones' killers accountable. In 1991, Baruso—who was allegedly paid $15,000 by the Marcos regime to orchestrate the murders—was finally found guilty of first-degree murder. He was ordered to pay millions to the victims' families, and died in prison in 2008.

Shockingly, the committee's legal work was also able to connect the murders directly to Marcos and his wife, Imelda. It was revealed that Gene and Silme's activism had frightened the dictator so badly that he sent gang members to murder them. The Marcoses were found liable by a federal jury in 1989 and ordered to pay $15 million to Gene and Silme's families. It marked the first and only time a foreign head of state has been held responsible for the deaths of Americans on American soil. With the families' blessing, Seattle's Northwest Labor and Employment Law Office used those funds to create the Domingo/Viernes Justice Fund in their memory.

Silme Domingo and Gene Viernes's memory still looms large. They have not been forgotten by Seattle's Filipino and labor communities, in the ILWU's storied history, or in the history of trailblazing rank-and-file Asian immigrant worker leaders in the U.S. labor movement. The Rank-and-File Committee they'd founded continued its reform mission. The beleaguered Local 37 eventually merged with the larger and more established Inlandboatmen's Union (IBU). Terri became vice president of Local 37 in 1981 and continued to work toward Silme's dream of reform. After the merger, she was elected the IBU's secretary treasurer in 1993. As of 2024, she still held the position.

The murders took a toll on an entire community, but they had an especially devastating impact on the two young daughters Silme left behind. Ligaya Domingo was only 3 years old when her father was murdered. She does not remember him as much as she would like but has kept his memory alive in her own way. She's spent her career in labor and devoted her life to uplifting vulnerable workers—just like her dad. She now works as the racial justice and education director at SEIU Healthcare 1199NW. "I was really instilled with the idea of needing to do work that changed the world," she told author Ron Chew in his oral history about her father and Gene. "Working in the labor movement in a lot of ways is like home to me, because I'm with people who understand me on this whole new level because they know my history."

Thanks to her and the many other workers who have drawn inspiration from their memory, Silme and Gene's dreams of achieving more equal labor standards and labor laws remain alive and well. In the end, even a dictator couldn't silence them.

Joni Christian
The True-to-Herself Trailblazer
1949–

It is my prayer to become the change I wish to see in the world.

Joni had butterflies in her stomach. It was her first day back at work after her big surgery, and she wasn't sure how well it was going to go. She hoped it would be fine. Maybe her boss would go easy on her as she continued to heal. Maybe her coworkers would understand. After all, they had worked together for years on the General Motors assembly line in Lordstown, Ohio. They knew she was a hard worker and a good friend. She had started working on the line in 1968, right after she finished high school. Some of the guys she worked with had probably gone to Ursuline High School with her in Youngstown, or attended the same Catholic church. They knew Joni—or at least, they thought they did.

What her coworkers didn't know was that when Joni turned 26, she began receiving hormone therapy. They definitely didn't know about her recent gender-affirming surgery yet. Today, they were about to find out that the person they'd worked alongside for over a decade was a transgender woman. Of course her transition hadn't changed anything about who she was as a person or how hard she worked on the assembly line. She could still handle the same heavy equipment and crack the same jokes. The biggest difference was that, for the first time in her life, Joni finally felt like herself. The image she showed the world finally matched who she was inside. It was 1975, and she was excited to get back to work and start her new life.

She showed up at work that day and nervously introduced herself to her coworkers using her new name—Joni Christian. Unfortunately, things didn't go as smoothly as she'd hoped. They didn't go well at all. Her coworkers and supervisors reacted very negatively. Some of it was ignorance; no one else at GM was openly LGBTQ then. It was normal for them to be curious and ask questions, and she had no problem with that. But some people reacted with pure prejudice. They didn't understand her journey and didn't want to try. The factory where she'd worked for nearly a decade became a hostile environment overnight. Joni was heartbroken.

She did not feel accepted and no longer even felt safe. She lost friends. Some coworkers ignored her or tried to exclude her from work events. Others even went out of their way to be hateful and harass her. "Women I worked with at General Motors Lordstown assembly plant circulated a petition to keep me out of the restroom," she remembered later. "Men stared and hurled cruel remarks." It was a painful situation, one that is still all too familiar to trans workers today. She felt like she was constantly being watched, whispered about, or sneered at. It all became too much for her to bear alone.

But she wasn't alone. Joni was also a member of the United Auto Workers Local 1112. She turned to her union for help and finally got the support she needed. Even if they didn't fully understand her story, the union leaders had her back because she was a union member. It was their job to advocate for every member—and thankfully, they did their job well. Given the way she was being treated by her coworkers and supervisors, she was able to use the union's legal services to sue GM for invasion of privacy. She won! After the company settled the lawsuit with her, conditions at work got a lot better. She could finally breathe again, even if she still wasn't as close to her coworkers as she had been. It was a lonely time to be a trailblazer, but Joni knew she deserved to live her life authentically. "The process of gender reassignment was my salvation, despite the ridicule, sarcasm, and shunning I experienced after I returned to the life I once lived as a man," she later explained.

The president of Local 1112, Gary Briner, was firmly in her corner. When Joni was working at GM, the vast majority of workers were men. Women were a rare sight on the assembly line, and gender nonconforming workers were an invisible minority. "We had only started having women working on the line in 1971, and we had to get tough then with how some of the men were acting," Briner explained. He was bothered by how some of the union's own members were behaving toward her. "So, women alone were a scarcity, let alone what Joni was doing. Some of the workers were acting like animals. But there were other brothers who were pretty embarrassed. She was paying dues, she had the right to do whatever she wanted."

The union's support meant everything to Joni. "The union taught me that an injury to one was an injury to all," she wrote later. Local 1112 continued to protect her from discrimination on the job and stood up for her whenever she needed them. "Returning to work after undergoing gender reassignment surgery was challenging," she reflected. "I would've been fired, if not for the union. The union respected me as a person, even if some of the members didn't approve of me." And even though she had to fight them for proper treatment, she also appreciated her job at GM, which paid well enough to cover the medical costs for her transition. She continued working there for many more years. Joni retired in 1999 after spending 31 years on the line—24 of them as her true self.

In her retirement, Joni found her way back to religion and became ordained as a lay minister. She's now very active in The Church in Silver Lake in Silver Lake, Ohio. She acts as the Minister of Extravagant Welcome, ensuring that people of all gender identities feel comfortable coming to the church. The issue of trans rights is very important to her, and she wants to do what she can to ensure no one ever feels as alone as she did that first day back at GM. Joni knows that not every religious organization shares her inclusive mission, but she is determined to be as welcoming and supportive as she wishes her coworkers had been in 1975. "God is a God of Love and not a god of hate," she says. "It has become my life's work. It is my prayer to become the change I wish to see in the world."

By taking on GM and demanding to be treated with respect, Joni set an important precedent. She transitioned during a time when LGBTQ people were openly discriminated against and often forced to hide who they were. A lot of time has passed, but many of the challenges she faced at GM are still a problem for many trans people in the workplace now. Trans people are three times more likely than the general population to be unemployed, and twice as likely to live in poverty. Those who find employment are at risk of being fired or discriminated against because of their identities, especially in states with anti-trans laws. Joni knew she could count on her union; now, a union contract is still the best protection that trans workers have to keep them safe on the job.

"Not everyone has a [u]nion but everyone deserves to have confidence that whatever their gender expression is, they should be able to get up and go to work without fearing that their livelihood will be taken from them," Joni wrote in 2015. Unions have plenty of room to improve, but they can still do a lot for their trans members. For example, they can bargain for contracts that ensure their members have access to gender-affirming healthcare. As Joni showed, they can also offer legal support when an employer (or a person's own coworkers) creates an unsafe working environment for them. There is still much to be done to ensure trans workers everywhere have the support they need. Organizing a union can be an important first step—and so can getting existing unions to step up. In 2021, the UAW announced the formation of a UAW LGBTQ caucus. Like Joni, the next generation of LGBTQ auto workers will be able to count on having a powerful ally in their corner if they need it.

"The world is coming to an understanding that God's beautiful humanity is very diverse," Joni said. "Lesbian, gay, bisexual, and transgender people are telling the world that we are part of all societies and will settle for nothing less than respect. When we tell the next generation that it really does get better, we have to stand up and tell our stories so that their stories will be respected as well."

Bhairavi Desai
Driven to Win
1973–

Their struggle has given my life purpose.

It was a blustery day in New York City, and a crowd of about two dozen taxi drivers filled the sidewalk. The wind carried the workers' chants up to the skyscrapers above them. They were holding a protest outside the headquarters for a company that had been ripping them off for years. "Shame! Shame! Shame!" they cried, waving signs and honking their horns. People walking by stopped to take flyers explaining the protest. In the middle of all the action stood a small woman with a cloud of gray hair and a colorful dress. She held up a bullhorn, her voice rising along with the taxi drivers'. As the protest wound down, drivers drifted over and formed a loose circle around her. Smiling, she put the bullhorn on the ground. They all leaned in to listen to her speak, and to add their own opinions. Together, they made a plan to hold another protest a few weeks later. The woman hugged a few of the drivers as they made their way back to their cars, shouting out a few last words of advice as she prepared to leave. The woman's name was Bhairavi Desai, and she was not only the taxi drivers' biggest supporter—she was the president of their union.

The drivers were all members of the New York Taxi Workers Alliance (NYTWA). The union represents 21,000 members throughout the city. The NYTWA advocates for their needs, lobbies for their interests, provides a wide array of resources, and helps them deal with financial problems. It's not a traditional labor union, but that's one of the reasons it works so well for this particular group of workers. They are a deeply diverse group in many ways but one. Ninety percent of Bhairavi's members were born in another country and they speak dozens of different languages, but over 95 percent of them are men. People don't always expect the leader of such a union to look like Bhairavi, but anyone who underestimates her is making a huge mistake. She is a lion in sheep's clothing (or, more accurately, a pink dress).

Bhairavi was born in Gujarat, India, and moved to the United States with her family when she was six years old. They landed in Harrison, New Jersey, where her mother found work in a factory, and her father opened a small grocery store. He had been a lawyer in India, but had to switch careers when they arrived in the U.S. His well-stocked shop became a community hub. His friends would come by to talk politics, and Bhairavi loved to listen in.

She had plenty of opportunities to do so, since it seemed as though he never left the counter. Her father worked seven days a week. He only ever closed the store for three reasons: funerals, to take Bhairavi to her after-school job, or if a family member or a neighbor needed help. Thanks to her father, Bhairavi learned all about hard work, fairness, and solidarity when she was still very young. It's also when she first began learning about liberation.

Her grandparents had been involved in the Indian liberation movement against the British. Rebellion was a family tradition. Bhairavi's grandmother proudly told her stories about being arrested while marching for freedom. Her own parents ensured that she understood the importance of their family history, too. She was raised knowing that it was important to fight for justice at home and everywhere. That lesson was reinforced every time she turned on the news. Growing up in New Jersey in the 1980s meant that there were always political events unfolding on the television. Bhairavi would watch news programs about the Sandinista revolution in Nicaragua and could tell that the news anchors wanted her to disapprove of the rebels. Instead, she felt nothing but empathy. "I didn't see a threat, I saw people that looked like me," she said. "I just felt such a deep sense of solidarity. It put my own class experience in perspective, my own experience of poverty in the first world."

Bhairavi later went to Rutgers University, where she majored in women's studies. After she graduated, she knew she wanted to use her degree to help women in need. She got a job with Manavi, a South Asian women's organization. Many of the women she worked with were immigrants who had been brought to the U.S. and then abandoned. She listened to their stories, offered resources, and gave them the support they needed to build new lives. The job required a big heart and an enormous amount of empathy, but Bhairavi had plenty of both to share.

Then, when she was 23, she became involved in the Committee to End Anti-Asian Violence, a group that provided social services to South Asian taxi drivers. It was a good fit for Bhairavi at first. She had always wanted to be an organizer, and the group had a lot of interesting ideas for ways to improve the drivers' lives. Not all of it sounded right to Bhairavi, though. She began to have disagreements with other members of the group about tactics and strategy. The issue came to a head when they formed the Lease Drivers Coalition. Her coworkers wanted to form a coalition group to bring drivers and customers together. But Bhairavi's goal for the project was different. She wanted to help the drivers form their own labor union. She wasn't interested in making friends with businesses, she wanted the workers to win!

The two conflicting approaches were never going to

work out, so in 1998, she left the group to work on something that made more sense to her. She and Javaid Tariq, who had worked with her at her old job and left for the same reasons, founded a brand-new organization—the New York Taxi Workers Alliance. Bhairavi has served as the union's leader ever since. They managed to start off with a bang, too. In May of that year, New York City mayor Rudy Guiliani announced a new set of costly fines targeting taxi drivers. In response, Bhairavi and the NYTWA decided to call the union's first strike. They gave themselves 10 days to plan it out, pulled a few all-nighters to get everything ready, then hoped for the best. Their members answered the call and responded loud and clear. In a move that our labor hero Judy Heumann would have recognized, thousands of drivers came together to block traffic and shut down Manhattan's streets for 24 hours to protest the new rules. That one was only a partial victory; they ultimately weren't able to stop the new fines from coming into effect, but they certainly made themselves heard (and gave Giuliani a monster headache!). That strike would be the first of many. Over the years, Bhairavi and the taxi drivers have taken on the city time and time again. Sometimes they've won big, other times they've lost, but each time they've given the fight everything they have. And Bhairavi has always been there to lead the charge.

Taxi drivers have had a tough time making ends meet

since 2014. That's when ridesharing apps like Uber and Lyft came in and scooped up many of their customers. The sharp increase in competition made it hard for the cab drivers to keep up. The yellow cab system in New York City has also placed drivers in a lot of debt. Some drivers took out loans worth hundreds of thousands of dollars to buy a taxi medallion (the official license that allows them to operate). The medallions were once valued at $1.2 million and seen as a smart investment for a worker's future, but when the apps came in, those medallions lost most of their value. The worst part was that all the drivers who had bought them were still left with all the debt. Thousands of people were suddenly struggling extra hard to make ends meet while also dealing with the heavy burden of financial debt. Many drivers felt completely hopeless. They had worked so hard to buy their licenses, and all of a sudden, poof! Their investment was worthless.

The NYTWA knew that its members could not bear to go on this way for very much longer. In 2021, Bhairavi led her members down to City Hall, where they spent 30 straight days protesting. Yellow cabs are an iconic symbol of the city, but they don't move without the drivers. If New York wanted to keep its taxis running, it was going to have to help their drivers. The city came out and offered them some financial relief, but it wasn't nearly enough. It seemed like the city government didn't understand how dire the situation actually was. Seeing that nothing was going to get done unless they took charge themselves, NYTWA came up with a new proposal that would bring real relief to the drivers without costing the city much money. It was a good solution for a complex problem, yet no one seemed to want to listen. They tried and tried to get Mayor Bill de Blasio to pay attention. Finally, they decided it was time for something more drastic.

On October 20, Bhairavi, NYTWA members, and their supporters hauled a bunch of tents and chairs over to City Hall, sat down, and stopped eating. Their hunger strike became front-page news, and sympathetic New Yorkers came down to City Hall to support them. For two weeks, they sat, living on only water and coconut water. The hunger strike went on and on, until finally, on November 3, they reached a deal with the city. Their painful action had been worth it: the drivers would get their loans reduced. They would get their chance to escape poverty. They had won! It was the union's biggest victory yet. Bhairavi just smiled as everyone celebrated around her. She'd never doubted for a moment that they would win.

The members respect her toughness, but there is also real love and affection there. When Bhairavi first started trying to organize their industry, she was only 25 years old. Organizing isn't exactly a lucrative job, and she was barely scraping by financially when she started working with the drivers. When they found out that she was struggling, they started to bring her hot home-cooked meals to keep her strength up. They would collect money to help pay her bills. The drivers adopted her as family and treated her like a niece or little sister. That's when Bhairavi knew she had found the right job. "If there wasn't going to be a group of drivers that believed in my work enough to make sure I could keep a roof over my head and food in my belly, then I wouldn't have been the right organizer for that job," she said. They took care of her, and now she takes care of them. That burden may seem heavy, but to her, it's second nature. Family always comes first. She is even married to a driver, fellow union activist Victor Salazar. (When they go out, though, he takes the wheel; Bhairavi has never learned to drive!) All these years later, the drivers still call her Sister Bhairavi.

Bhairavi's personal politics have also been a major driver behind her work. Her loyalty has always been with the poor, the oppressed, and the exploited; it's in her blood. The taxi drivers she fights so fiercely for fall into that category. So did her own family when she was growing up. She didn't realize they were poor until she applied for college and was handed financial aid forms. Later on, when she was a young organizer, powerful people didn't bother taking her seriously. Politicians and city officials would refuse to meet with her. Instead of leaving, though, she would always stay, and talk with whoever was there, whether it was a staffer or the receptionist. It was her way of trying to build solidarity and get her message out. Now, those same big shots call asking *her* for meetings. "I understood they were trying to tell me that I was not worthy enough of their time, but I just could not walk away and look at an administrative assistant and say to them that they were not worthy of my time," she said. "I would have felt like somebody who looked down on the people I grew up with."

All these years in, Bhairavi is now the sort of person who calls press conferences. It's part of her job to entertain politicians, give interviews, and field endless media requests. She's a mover and shaker in the New York City labor movement. Given a choice, though, she still prefers to get work done behind the scenes. She can call the shots now but would still rather huddle up with a group of her members on a chilly street corner and make important decisions as a collective. To her, their movement is a community, and communities care for one another. Drivers are vulnerable, essential workers, invisible to nearly everyone, but Bhairavi Desai sees them. They see her, too, and will gladly follow her onto the battlefield as many times as it takes. Sister Desai is always ready to fight for her family. "They just work so hard, and there's just so much integrity, and I just love them so much," she said. "Their struggle has given my life purpose."

Jennifer Bates
The Faithful Leader
1972–

I will not be silenced. We will not be stopped.

Jennifer's legs were killing her today. She had been trying to ignore the pain all afternoon, but it just wouldn't stop. The dull throbbing radiated through her calves. She lifted another heavy box and sighed. All she wanted to do was go home and put her feet up, but her shift wasn't over for three more hours. She wasn't allowed to leave early no matter how badly she was hurting. It wasn't an option to slow her pace, either, because she would get in trouble. The managers watched Jennifer and her coworkers closely to make sure they were active for every second of their shift. When workers got in trouble, they lost time off or were written up by their managers. After three strikes, you were out. There was no room for mistakes.

All around her, hundreds of other workers busied themselves lifting heavy boxes, filling packages, and hunting down items within the gigantic warehouse's shelves.

A lot of them were hurting, too. Theirs was a hard job with long hours, lots of physical activity, and few breaks to rest or use the bathroom. The company demanded that they keep moving, moving, moving—time was money, and their employers *really* liked money. No matter how tired or sore the workers were feeling, the orders just kept coming in. Jennifer sighed and turned back to her station. It was another day at Amazon, and she still had so much work to do. Time *was* money, after all, and she was being paid just $15.30 per hour for each ten-hour shift.

It's hard to describe just how powerful Amazon is, or how much money the company makes. It can feel like Amazon is everywhere and everything. It is a multinational corporation with hubs in multiple countries. It is an online retailer that sells anything and everything (how many times have you thought to yourself, "Oh, I'll just buy it on Amazon"?). Its web services power many of the websites we—and the U.S. government—use every day. It also sells its own products like Alexa, Kindle, Amazon Music, and Prime Video. It has experimented with opening its own brick-and-mortar retail stores. In 2017, Amazon bought Whole Foods, the upmarket grocery chain. It uses is own distribution services, like Amazon Fresh and Amazon Flex, to deliver more than 5 billion packages per year in the U.S. alone. Its smiling logo is as ubiquitous as that of McDonald's or Nike. Amazon delivery vans prowl countless neighborhoods each day, dropping off packages as Amazon Ring cameras silently watch everyone who walks by.

Amazon is probably one of the best-known companies in the world right now, but its reputation for quick service hasn't been able to mask the other major fact about the company. It has an absolutely terrible record on workplace safety and workers' rights. The U.S. Department of Labor has investigated Amazon multiple times for its unsafe working conditions. Its labor law violations continue to pile up, too, and the company has spent millions trying to bust up union drives at its physical locations. In the warehouses, workers have to deal with constant surveillance, insufficient break time, and physical exhaustion on the job; meanwhile, delivery drivers are pushed to drive at unsafe speeds and monitored by video cameras. The rapid pace and lack of rest that Amazon has become infamous for takes a terrible toll on the workers' physical and mental health. Workers have been seriously injured—or even killed—while on the job at Amazon. People have had heart attacks, suffered grievous injuries, and even collapsed in the bathroom. In November 2021, two workers at the Alabama warehouse where Jennifer works died on the same day. A month later, six workers were killed when a tornado demolished an Amazon warehouse in Edwardsville, Illinois. They had asked to go home when the weather report came in, but their supervisors refused.

Thanks to workers like them, Amazon made over $30 billion in profits in 2023. Its founder, Jeff Bezos, is one of the richest men in the world. His net worth is about $190 billion. In 2021, he spent $5.5 billion to fly to space for four minutes and bought a "superyacht" for $500 million. During that same year, Amazon employed a total of 1.1 million people in the U.S. The company has since become the country's second largest employer, after Walmart—another corporation with a long track record of union-busting. Amazon has locations all over the country, and 9,000 of their employees, including Jennifer, work at warehouses and other facilities in Alabama. Jennifer started working at Amazon's fulfillment center in Bessemer, Alabama, in 2020. Before that, she had spent a decade working at a nearby U.S. Pipe plant. Her sister was already working at Amazon when the COVID-19 pandemic hit in early 2020, and the Bessemer warehouse had opened in March of that year. By May, Bates had decided to join her there. She dropped off an application on her way to her factory job, and soon got a call offering her a job in Bessemer. They were eager to hire as many people as they could to get the warehouse up and running quickly. Jennifer thought it was worth giving it a shot. Amazon was offering decent wages and health insurance—how bad could it be?

The night before she started at Amazon, Jennifer sat in her car for two hours and cried. She was going to miss her friends at the plant and didn't know what to expect from her new employer. But somehow, she knew that that warehouse was where she needed to be. "I felt like I was leaving my family, but I knew it was something that I had to do," she explained. "When Spirit gives you a task, once you start on that task, ain't no turnin' around."

She was no stranger to hard work even before she got to Bessemer. Jennifer grew up in Marion, Alabama, a small city about an hour and half's drive from Bessemer. She got her first job when she was 13 years old, picking okra in a neighbor's field for a few dollars a week. At 16, she started working at a local Hardee's. Since then, Jennifer has worked in all kinds of places. Restaurants, in retail, as a combination 911 and police dispatcher, and in factories making automobile parts—she's tried 'em all, and always found a silver lining in even the toughest jobs. A warehouse gig sounded nice and straightforward compared to the stress of the dispatch or frantic pace at the factory. It didn't take her long to adjust to the demands of her Amazon job, as harsh as they were. It took her even less time to realize that changes needed to be made.

At Amazon, the workers had no protections at all besides basic labor laws (which the company wasn't very interested in anyway). Their executives knew that they could just keep hiring new people anytime someone complained. The wages they were offering were much better than many other employers in the area, and people were willing to put up with a whole lot of garbage to ensure they could make ends meet. They didn't have much choice. Squeaky wheels just got sent home. Amazon prefers to open its warehouses in places like Alabama for a reason: they assume they can get away with just about anything. Alabama's conservative state government is eager to attract new businesses and is openly hostile to unions. When workers complain, the people in power pretend not to hear them. Meanwhile, wealthy employers like Amazon are welcomed as valued investors.

That's what happened in Bessemer. It used to be a thriving industrial center but is now one of the poorest cities in Alabama. About 30 percent of its residents live below the poverty line. There are not many economic opportunities in the area, and the state's hourly minimum wage is still only $7.25. Since Amazon pays a $15 starting hourly wage, the company attracts as many workers as it needs. The employee turnover rate (i.e., the number of workers leaving and new ones coming in) is 150 percent, which is double the industry average. The fact that workers rush to escape so quickly should be a clue to everyone watching that something very wrong is happening behind that Amazon logo.

Even with all those odds stacked against it, Jennifer was convinced that there was something that could be done to improve their situation. She wasn't the only one who thought that, either. When her coworker Daryl Richardson asked if she'd be interested in trying to organize a union at Amazon, she was all in. At Jennifer's last job, she had the benefit of a union to handle problems on the shop floor; U.S. Pipe was unionized, and Jennifer was a member of their Steelworkers local. She saw firsthand the difference a union contract could make in wages and working conditions and wanted the same for her new coworkers at Amazon.

During the early days of their union drive, when most of the workers were still nervous about putting themselves out there, Jennifer jumped in feet first. She became a public face of the campaign and discovered that she was also an extremely effective organizer. Her people skills and varied work experience were exactly the right tools for the job. Alongside the other workers on their committee, Jennifer and Daryl spent countless hours talking to other Amazon workers about the union. She answered their questions and soothed their fears. Unionizing was a new concept to some of her coworkers, but she explained why she thought that was the best way forward. In her view, Amazon needed to be held accountable. She and her coworkers needed to have their voices heard, no matter the costs. "I said, you know what, I'm not running," said Jennifer. "I've seen people being mistreated. I've seen people just get fired. When is it gonna stop?"

By the summer, the workers had gone public with their intention to form a union with the Retail, Wholesale and Department Store Union (RWDSU). If successful, their union would have been the first in Amazon's entire U.S. operation. As it stood, the very fact that they went public with their union drive was a huge inspiration for the hundreds of thousands of workers toiling in the company's 800 other U.S. warehouse facilities. Bessemer wasn't the first place that workers had tried to organize; they were building on past efforts. Though Amazon CEO Jeff Bezos's goons cracked down on them wherever possible, some small gains had been made by workers in other places. It seemed like the dominos were ready to fall. Everyone knew it would take something big and bold and visionary to finally crack Amazon's seemingly impenetrable armor. Alabama was the last place that people expected to look, but that moment came in 2021. A group of middle-aged Black warehouse workers in a struggling Alabama exurb, whose union roots run as deep as the coal mines outside its borders, had decided to take on the giant.

Amazon fought back. A union was the last thing they wanted in their nice new warehouse; they worried that if those workers were able to unionize, others would want to do it too, and the company would lose some of the immense power it held over its workforce. The very thought made the executives shudder. In Bessemer, Amazon used every trick it could think of to try to intimidate workers, spread false information about the union, and convince them to vote "no" in the upcoming union election.

The RWDSU's organizers had an uphill battle ahead of them. The COVID-19 pandemic was still raging, and it was difficult for RWDSU organizers to connect with workers in person. Amazon would not allow them on company property, and it wasn't safe to hold large meetings or visit workers at their homes. There was also some red tape to get through. Amazon had refused to recognize their union when they went public, so the workers would be required to vote in a union election run by the National Labor Relations Board. This dragged out the timeline, giving Amazon more opportunities to spread anti-union messaging. Workers suspected that the election might not be fair, either. Amazon had secretly set up a mailbox outside the Bessemer warehouse and encouraged workers to drop their ballots inside. The problem was, no one knew who was checking the box or monitoring the votes. It all seemed very suspicious, and some workers got cold feet. They didn't want to risk their jobs by going against the boss. Amazon had even threatened to shut down the warehouse if the workers voted for a union. In spite of all the difficulties, Jennifer and the other organizers stayed hopeful.

When the final vote tally came out, though, the results were disappointing. Despite the organizers' best efforts, Amazon's anti-union campaign had won. The union drive had ended in a loss. It hadn't been a fair fight, though. RWDSU immediately filed almost two dozen charges against Amazon with the National Labor Relations Board, alleging a number of unfair labor practices. The board agreed with them, and ordered a second election to be run. That effort failed, too. Organizers again had to deal with many of the same issues that they faced the first time around. In addition, Amazon's high turnover rate meant that many of the workers who had voted in the second election had not even been working there during the original union drive. Jennifer and the other organizers basically had to redo the entire union drive from scratch.

While the workers at Jennifer's warehouse in Bessemer were locked in their battle with Amazon, another group of Amazon workers much farther north were launching a campaign of their own. It was led by worker-organizers Christian Smalls, Derrick Palmer, Michelle Valentin Nieves, and Angelika Maldonado at an Amazon warehouse in Staten Island, New York. They began organizing a few months after the Alabama union drive went public, inspired by the Alabamians' bravery. On April 1,

2022, the Amazon Labor Union made history by winning their union election. They proved that it could be done. Since then, Amazon workers in several other locations have tried to unionize their own facilities, and the Amazon Labor Union has officially affiliated with the powerful Teamsters union to continue fighting for a first contract.

Back in Alabama, Jennifer made it very clear that she and her coworkers weren't ready to give up on the dream of a union. After the second election result came out, they took time to mourn—and then continued to organize. As new waves of workers arrived at the Bessemer warehouse, pro-union workers showed them the ropes. Amazon's bad reputation as dangerous union-busters continued to grow, too. Jennifer gave interviews to the press, spoke at meetings with her coworkers, met with celebrities and politicians, and even testified in front of Congress about Amazon's anti-union practices. She had become a star, for good reason. Amazon knew that they couldn't break her spirit or make her give up. So in the summer of 2023, the company decided to try a new tactic.

Jennifer had long suffered health problems due to the physical demands of her job at Amazon. After the pain became too much for her to bear, she filed for workers' compensation and was granted a medical leave of absence. While she finally began to heal, she held on to every piece of documentation—just in case. When Amazon ordered her to return to work, they made it as difficult as possible for her. Her doctor had emphasized her need to avoid the repetitive motions that had led to her injuries in the first place, but Amazon refused to make any accommodations or changes to her work schedule. She was sent right back to the packing line. Jennifer steeled herself and did as they asked. The pain came roaring back, and Amazon sent her home to get a new doctor's review. Paperwork in hand, she came back to work, only to discover that she had been fired. They had finally figured out how to get rid of her and wasted no time in doing so. It felt like a punch in the stomach. "I've given my back to Amazon these past three years," she told reporters. "I've given my arms and shoulders to Amazon these past three years. And I've given every fiber of my soul into organizing Amazon these past three years. For them to treat me like this is unfathomable."

The bad publicity forced the company to address her termination. At first, Amazon's HR department insisted that the issue concerned her taking unpaid time off. Jennifer came back with receipts. She had kept all the documentation showing that she had been granted medical leave. Amazon changed their story again and told RWDSU president Stuart Appelbaum that she had been "subjected to termination by AI due to a glitch in the company's own software." In short, it was Amazon's mistake, not hers, but she still had to appeal her termination. With RWDSU's help, she also filed an unfair labor practice charge with the National Labor Relations Board. When the news became public, Jennifer received an outpouring of support from workers around the world, and Amazon was flooded with criticism. After two weeks, Jennifer got her job back. "Amazon was wrong, they tried to fire me and stifle a movement, but the movement pushed back, and I'm incredibly humbled by the global outpouring of support for my unjust termination," she told her supporters. "If there's a lesson to be learned it's that today Amazon workers everywhere now know that when you're under attack, you have to stand up and fight back, because when we fight, clearly, we win!"

The David-and-Goliath fight that has consumed her time and attention for years has never consumed her spirit. If anything, the continual setbacks have made her even more determined to win. Like so many other labor leaders before her, Jennifer has given everything she has to the cause, and she's not finished yet. "We are a movement, and I know my union, recognized or not by you, has my back," she warned Amazon. "I will not be silenced. We will not be stopped."

Labor's Next Chapter

Journalists are given the power to decide whose stories are told and whose are forgotten. It's a big responsibility that carries heavy consequences. The choices we make as writers, journalists, historians, and other story-savers influence the way history itself is created. Digging up information on the past can sometimes feel like going on a treasure hunt where you've only got half of the map. It takes a lot of work to find out what—or who—is lying below the surface, just waiting for you to bring them back into the spotlight. I did a lot of that when I was writing the adult version of this book, *Fight Like Hell: The Untold History of Labor*, and I was so happy when I got the opportunity to write this version.

I'm also so grateful to all the brilliant historians, academic researchers, archivists, and journalists over the centuries who have preserved the precious details of these labor heroes' lives and ensured that we won't forget their stories. There have been and continue to be so many fascinating people involved in the American labor movement that *Fight to Win!* could have been hundreds of pages longer. Think of the stories in this book as a beginner's guide, or an intro class. Now that you've met some of them, you can dive even deeper into their lives by reading more about them and the context in which they lived (don't worry—I've added a list of sources and suggested reading to get you started!).

We're now living in a moment of enormous energy and enthusiasm for unions and workers' rights. Ever since the beginning of the COVID-19 pandemic, many people's relationships with work have changed. They began to question why it felt like their safety didn't matter, and why they were risking their lives for low wages. The urgency and uncertainty of the pandemic threw an even harsher spotlight on the desperate realities of work in this country—especially for those who didn't have the option to stay home. When the arrival of COVID-19 vaccines lessened the immediate threat of the pandemic, bosses saw no reason to keep pretending they valued their employees' role in keeping the country running (if they'd ever been bothered to do so in the first place) or raise their stagnating wages. As this all played out, the government continued to bolster the fortunes of the rich and fail everyone else. The American working class was being brought to its breaking point, and something had to give. "People are angry and fed up," my friend Veena Dubal, Professor of Law at the University of California, Irvine School of Law, told me as I was writing the adult version of this book. "I don't think that we can discount the role that those emotions play in the uprisings that we've seen among workers in this country [in 2021]."

As the year went on, the workers communicated that fact in no uncertain terms. Thousands took advantage of a tight labor market to walk away from low-paid, high-risk jobs. They marched on bad bosses, struck at callous, crooked corporations, and used their collective power to push back against a ruthless system that expected them to cheerfully accept exploitation with a smile. Some dubbed it "The Great Resignation," others insisted it was a slow-burning general strike. "After years of being underserved and taken for granted—& doubly so during the pandemic—workers are starting to authorize strikes across the country," Rep. Alexandria Ocasio-Cortez observed on Twitter. "Good."

Either way, it happened everywhere, even in places one might not expect. In Alabama, for example, after the Amazon workers in Bessemer lost their union vote at the end of March, they won an appeal against the company's flagrant union-busting, and immediately began making plans to rerun the election. RWDSU organizer Michael "Big Mike" Foster celebrated in a tweet—"Here we go again, but this time with a win!"—and immediately got back to work. Meanwhile, coal miners in Brookwood went on strike for almost two years straight as they battled Warrior Met Coal to win a fair union contract. Out on an unfair labor practices strike against a company that seemed hellbent on starving them out instead of negotiating a decent contract, the miners faced an uphill climb, but it was nothing the United Mine Workers of America (UMWA) hadn't dealt with before. As you've already read, miners are tough, resourceful, and stubborn. We didn't even get into the Battle of Blair Mountain, the union's epic 15-month strike against Massey Coal in 1985, or the role the fearless miner's wife and expert saboteur Sarah "Ma" Blizzard played in the brutal 1912 Paint-Creek Cabin Creek strike, but trust me—you wouldn't want to find yourself on their bad side.

As Alabama's craven Republican politicians did their darndest to hamstring any whisper of progress, a group of miners' spouses and retirees sprang into action to support their loved ones on the line. Like Ah Quon McElrath, Mother Jones, and so many of our other labor heroes, these women realized that it would take everyone pitching in. They quickly built a mutual aid network that fed hundreds of union families each week and led a holiday toy drive to bring a little joy to the next generation. "We're not just going to stand there silent on the sidelines and be at home with the kids in the kitchen," Haeden Wright, a high school teacher and president of the UMWA Auxiliary in Brookwood, whose husband Braxton was involved in the strike, told me that August. "The company needs to know that when a man works for Warrior Met, the entire family signs that contract. And women can be a whole lot more vicious when you attack our families than men can."

Despite their very best efforts, though, they didn't win their strike. Those miners—the ones who returned to Warrior Met, anyway—still haven't settled a new union contract with the company. It's not much of a happy ending, but there's a lesson in there. The workers don't always win. The movement can break your heart, but that's no reason to give up on trying anyway. The Brookwood miners are still negotiating and the Amazon workers in Bessemer are still fighting to win their union. In 2024, the mighty United Auto Workers arrived to try to unionize several automakers just down the road from Bessemer.

Alabama's labor movement was once again in the eye of a storm—and once again, forces outside the organizers' control contributed to yet another loss. At the time of this writing, the UAW has filed an objection to the vote at Mercedes, saying that the company interfered with the election by intimidating potential union voters. We'll have to see how that one plays out, but the one thing we know for sure is that none of them—the miners, the Amazon workers, or the autoworkers—would dream of giving up without a fight. It may take years, or even decades, but as history has shown us, the good guys always win . . . eventually. In Alabama, in Arkansas, in Alaska, and everywhere else, the most important thing to remember is to never stop trying.

And that's also kind of the point of all this, right? History does not stop just because one strike ends, or one campaign wraps up, or one stressed-out writer needs to hit her deadline. There is always another fight, a new contract, a fresh adversary. There is always another struggle to join, and another picket line to walk. Labor's work is never done. Collective working-class power is behind every step forward this country has made. Once you've committed to the idea of building a better world, you can't clock out of the fight for justice.

People have been dreaming of ways to build a better world since the moment we appeared on this planet. Thanks to the labor movement, we have made incredible progress in many areas of our society, but there is still a lot of work to be done to get to where we need to be. The people you've met in this book understood that they might not win everything they wanted, but they could at least try to push things a little bit further ahead. Bit by bit, day by day, year by year, they and their descendants have seen some of those dreams come true, from the eight-hour workday to a federal minimum wage to laws against child labor. If they hadn't dreamed as big and fought as hard as they did, our world would look a lot different—and honestly, it would be a whole lot worse. Thanks to those who came before us, we now have the opportunity to build upon the work they did and leave the world in better shape than we found it.

Some of the stories in this book may have broken your heart. Some may have made you laugh, or shake your head, or raise your fist in triumph. The people within these pages were tough, determined, messy, and complicated human beings just like you and me. They weren't perfect, they made mistakes, they lost campaigns and caused trouble. They also cared deeply about their fellow workers, and refused to back down when it felt like the entire world was against them.

I hope you find inspiration in their stories, and take the lessons they taught us to heart. *Fight to Win!*'s goal is to educate a new generation of workers on their rights, their history, and the sacrifices that so many people have made to get us to this imperfect point. I also hope that the stories you've read here will inspire you to take action if you spot a bad boss or see your rights being stomped on. If everyone you've met in this book could do it, anyone can. *You* can.

If you've got a few friends ready to fight right along with you, anything is possible. *¡Sí, se puede!*

ACKNOWLEDGMENTS

First, I have to thank my amazing editor, Krista Vitola, for believing in this project. Not only is she a thoughtful, wise, and meticulous editor, she is also deeply kind and endlessly patient. I'm endlessly grateful to have gotten to work on this book with her. My phenomenal literary agent slash book dad, Chad Luibl at Janklow & Nesbit, was there for me every step of the way, too, and is the reason this book even exists in the first place. A couple of years ago, I randomly texted him, "What if I did a kids' version of *Fight Like Hell?*" He replied, "Let's make it happen!" And so we did.

Eternal thanks also to the entire Simon & Schuster Children's production and marketing team for working their magic (and putting up with my wacky ideas). Jennifer Strada, Chava Wolin, and Tara Shanahan, you're all beautiful geniuses and I appreciate you so much. The same goes for everyone at One Signal, Atria, and Simon & Schuster who worked on my first book, *Fight Like Hell: The Untold History of American Labor*—none of this would have happened without your brilliance and support. My eternal thanks to everyone who bought a copy, borrowed one from a friend or your local library, came to an event, or gave it a nice review. It has meant more than you know.

I am also massively indebted to all of the incredible authors, academics, historians, archivists, journalists, organizers, and rank-and-file workers without whose labor, perspectives, and insights were so critical to my research for this book: thank you for what you do. I am especially grateful to filmmakers like Laurie Coyle and historians like Peter Cole, Judy Yung, Melinda Chateauvert, Yevette Richards, Jaqueline Jones, Kirsten Downey, Ron Chew, and many more for going above and beyond to rediscover and preserve the stories of marginalized figures. Thank you to Haymarket Books, AK Press, PM Press, and Verso for publishing so many great labor books (and for hooking me up with research copies!), and to the saintly library workers at the Free Library of Philadelphia for letting me bury you in interlibrary loan requests. My deepest gratitude to *The Nation*, *Lux Magazine*, and *Vox*, where earlier versions of some of these stories appeared. Special thanks to Jennifer Bates and Bhairavi Desai for letting me interview you over the years and allowing me to share your stories with a new generation of troublemakers—you're *my* labor heroes.

And finally, thank you, thank you, thank you to all my dear friends and family for putting up with my chaotic schedule and loving me anyway, and to my devastatingly handsome other half, Shawn, for all of your unwavering support, enthusiastic encouragement, and well-timed sweet treats. I love you.

CHAPTER SOURCES

Sarah Bagley

Arnesen, Eric. *The Human Tradition in American Labor History*. Wilmington, Delaware: SR Books, 2004.

Cruea, Susan M. "Changing Ideals of Womanhood During the Nineteenth-Century Woman Movement." *American Transcendental Quarterly* 19, no. 3 (September 2005): 187. https://scholarworks.bgsu.edu/cgi/viewcontent.cgi?article=1000&context=gsw_pub.

DeFrancesco, Joey La Neve. "Pawtucket, America's First Factory Strike." Jacobin, June 6, 2018. https//jacobin.com/2018/06/factory-workers-strike-textile-mill-women.

"Factory Girls' Association." St. James Encyclopedia of Labor History Worldwide: Major Events in Labor History and Their Impact. Encyclopedia.com, November 13, 2024. www.encyclopedia.com/history/encyclopedias-almanacs-transcripts-and-maps/factory-girls-association.

Foner, Philip Sheldon, ed. *The Factory Girls: A Collection of Writings on Life and Struggles in the New England Factories of the 1840s*. University of Illinois Press eBooks, 1977. ci.nii.ac.jp/ncid/BA05124842.

Moran, William. *The Belles of New England: The Women of the Textile Mills and the Families Whose Wealth They Wove*. New York: St. Martin's Press, 2002. ci.nii.ac.jp/ncid/BA6681536X.

"The Role of Women in the Industrial Revolution." Tsongas Industrial History Center. UMass Lowell. Accessed December 10, 2021. https://www.uml.edu/Tsongas/barilla-taylor/women-industrial-revolution.aspx.

"Sarah Bagley." Lowell National Historical Park (U.S. National

Park Service). Accessed November 22, 2022. http://www.nps.gov/lowe/learn/historyculture/sarah-bagley.htm.

"Sarah Bagley Avenges the New England Mill Girls." New England Historical Society, April 18, 2022. https://newenglandhistoricalsociety.com/sarah-bagley-avenges-new-england-mill-girls.

Ben Fletcher

Cole, Peter. *Ben Fletcher: The Life and Times of a Black Wobbly*. Oakland, CA: PM Press, 2021.

Cole, Peter. "IWW Local 8: Philadelphia's Interracial Longshore Union." The Great Depression in Washington State Project. Accessed November 22, 2022. https://depts.washington.edu/iww/local8iww.shtml.

Cole, Peter. "Philadelphia's Lords of the Docks: Interracial Unionism Wobbly-Style." *The Journal of the Gilded Age and Progressive Era* 6, no. 3 (July 2007): 311–38. https://doi.org/10.1017/s1537781400002115.

Parfitt, Steven. "The Justice Department Campaign Against the IWW, 1917–1920." The Great Depression in Washington State Project. Accessed November 22, 2022. https://depts.washington.edu/iww/justice_dept.shtml#_edn2.

Roos, Dave. "The Sedition and Espionage Acts Were Designed to Quash Dissent During WWI." History.com, August 25, 2023. https://www.history.com/news/sedition-espionage-acts-woodrow-wilson-wwi.

Seraile, William. "Ben Fletcher, I.W.W. Organizer." *Pennsylvania History: A Journal of Mid-Atlantic Studies* 46, no. 3 (July 1979): 213–32.

Clara Lemlich

"Clara Lemlich and the Uprising of the 20,000." *American Experience*, PBS, August 10, 2017. www.pbs.org/wgbh/americanexperience/features/biography-clara-lemlich.

Dwyer, Jim. "Triangle Fire: One Woman Who Changed

the Rules." City Room, March 25, 2011. https://archive.nytimes.com/cityroom.blogs.nytimes.com/2011/03/22/one-woman-who-changed-the-rules.

Kennedy, Susan Estabrook, and Philip S. Foner. "Women and the American Labor Movement: From World War I to the Present." *Journal of American History*. 68, no. 2 (September 1981): 424. https://doi.org/10.2307/1890048.

Lemlich, Clara. "Testimonials: 'Life in the Shop.'" Cornell University ILR School, Remembering the 1911 Triangle Factory Fire. Accessed August 29, 2024. https://trianglefire.ilr.cornell.edu/primary/testimonials/ootss_ClaraLemlich.html.

Martin, Douglas. "Rose Freedman, Last Survivor of Triangle Fire, Dies at 107." *New York Times*, February 17, 2001. https://www.nytimes.com/2001/02/17/nyregion/rose-freedman-last-survivor-of-triangle-fire-dies-at-107.html.

Michels, Tony. "Uprising of 20,000 (1909)." Jewish Women's Archive. https://jwa.org/encyclopedia/article/uprising-of-20000-1909.

Shepherd, William. "Testimonials: 'Eyewitness at the Triangle.'" Cornell University ILR School, Remembering the 1911 Triangle Factory Fire. Accessed November 19, 2022. https://trianglefire.ilr.cornell.edu/primary/testimonials/ootss_WilliamShepherd.html.

Stein, Leon. "Lament for Lives Lost: Rose Schneiderman and the Triangle Fire." History Matters. Accessed November 19, 2022. https://historymatters.gmu.edu/d/5480.

Frances Perkins

Breitman, Jessica. "Frances Perkins: Honoring the Achievements of FDR's Secretary of Labor." FDR Presidential Library and Museum. https://www.fdrlibrary.org/perkins.

"Frances Perkins." National Park Service. https://www.nps.gov/people/frances-perkins.htm.

Gibbons, Chip. "The Trial(s) of Harry Bridges." Jacobin, September 15, 2016. https://jacobin.com/2016/09/harry-bridges-longshore-strike-deportation-communist-party.

"Hall of Honor Inductee: Frances M. Perkins." U.S. Department of Labor. https://www.dol.gov/general/aboutdol/hallofhonor/1989_perkins.

"Her Life: The Woman Behind the New Deal." Frances Perkins Center. https://francesperkinscenter.org/learn/her-life.

King, Loren. "Maine's Frances Perkins Center Gives FDR's New Deal Architect Her Due." *Boston Spirit Magazine*, May 11, 2021. https://bostonspiritmagazine.com/2021/05/maines-frances-perkins-center-gives-fdrs-new-deal-architect-her-due.

Lucy Parsons

Jones, Jacqueline. *Goddess of Anarchy: The Life and Times of Lucy Parsons, American Radical*. London: Hachette UK, 2017.

"Life Story: Lucy Parsons." Women & the American Story. Accessed August 29, 2024. https://wams.nyhistory.org/industry-and-empire/labor-and-industry/lucy-parsons/.

"Lucy Parsons: Woman of Will." Industrial Workers of the World. Accessed August 29, 2024. https://archive.iww.org/history/biography/LucyParsons/1/.

Parsons, Lucy E. "To Tramps." The Anarchist Library. https://theanarchistlibrary.org/library/lucy-e-parsons-to-tramps.

Rosenthal, Keith. "More Dangerous Than a Thousand Rioters." SocialistWorker.org, September 22, 2011. https://socialistworker.org/2011/09/22/lucy-parsons.

Mother Jones

Friedman, Gail. "March of the Mill Children." *Encyclopedia of Greater Philadelphia*, April 9, 2022. https://philadelphiaencyclopedia.org/essays/march-of-the-mill-children.

Gorn, Elliot J. "The History of Mother Jones." *Mother Jones*. Accessed August 29, 2024. https://www.motherjones.com/about/history.

Gorn, Elliott J. *Mother Jones: An American Life*. New York: Farrar, Straus and Giroux, 2015.

Hammond, Adam. "Ludlow Massacre survivor turns 104." *Denver 7 Colorado News (KMGH)*, January 13, 2018. https://www.denver7.com/thenow/ludlow-massacre-survivor-turns-104.

Horne, Madison. "These Appalling Images Exposed Child Labor in America." History.com, August 11, 2023. https://www.history.com/news/child-labor-lewis-hine-photos.

Kahle, Trish. "A Woman's Place Is in the Umwa: Women Miners and the Struggle for a Democratic Union in Western Pennsylvania, 1973–1979. *Labor* 13, no. 1 (February 1, 2016): 41–63. doi: https://doi.org/10.1215/15476715-3341058.

Kerr, Charles, and Hakan Erbil. "The Autobiography of Mother Jones." Industrial Workers of the World. Accessed August 29, 2024. https://archive.iww.org/history/library/MotherJones/autobiography/.

"Mother Jones." AFL-CIO. Accessed August 20, 2023. https://aflcio.org/about/history/labor-history-people/mother-jones.

Raye, Janet. "Hellraisers Journal: Whereabouts and Doings of Mother Jones for November 1900, Part IV: Found With Silk Strikers of Wilkes-Barre & Carbondale, Pennsylvania." *Hellraisers Journal*, December 20, 2020. https://weneverforget.org/hellraisers-journal-whereabouts-doings-of-mother-jones-for-november-1900-part-iv-found-with-silk-strikers-of-wilkes-barre-carbondale-pennsylvania.

Stepenoff, Bonnie. "Child Labor in Pennsylvania's Silk Mills: Protest and Change, 1900–1910." *Pennsylvania History: A Journal of Mid-Atlantic Studies* 59, no. 2 (1992): 101–21. Accessed August 29, 2024. http://www.jstor.org/stable/27773524.

Stepenoff, Bonnie. "Keeping It in the Family: Mother Jones and the Pennsylvania Silk Strike of 1900–1901." *Labor History*, 38, no. 4 (1997): 432–449. https://doi.org/10.1080/00236649712331387214.

Eugene V. Debs

Bly, Nellie. "Interview with Eugene V. Debs at Woodstock Jail." *New York World*, January 19, 1895. https://www.marxists.org/archive/debs/works/1895/950119-bly-debsatwoodstock.pdf.

"Debs Biography." The Eugene V. Debs Foundation. Accessed August 27, 2023. https://debsfoundation.org/index.php/landing/debs-biography.

Debs, Euguene. "Eugene Debs: The Red Flag 'Is a Sign of Terror to Every Tyrant.'" Jacobin, June 26, 2021. https:// jacobin.com/2021/06/eugene-debs-socialism-red-flag.

Debs, Katherine Metzel. "Kate Debs on the 'Right of Women to Vote.'" March 8, 2022. https://jacobin.com/2022/03/kate-debs-international-womens-day-socialism-suffrage-radical-politics.

"Eugene Debs: Topics in Chronicling America: Introduction." Library of Congress Research Guides. Accessed August 27, 2023. https://guides.loc.gov/chronicling-america-eugene-debs.

"Fellow Worker Eugene V Debs." Industrial Workers of the World. Accessed August 29, 2024. https://archive.iww.org/history/biography/EugeneDebs/1/.

"Gene Debs and the American Railway Union." Illinois Labor History Society, January 23, 2016. www.illinoislaborhistory.org/labor-history-articles/gene-debs-and-the-american-railway-union.

Ginger, Ray. *The Bending Cross: A Biography of Eugene Victor Debs*. New York: Russell & Russell Publishers, 1969.

"The Strike of 1894." National Park Service. Accessed August 24, 2023. www.nps.gov/pull/learn/historyculture/the-strike-of-1894.htm.

Rosina Tucker

"The Alliance That Began with the Brotherhood." American Postal Workers Union, January 27, 2003. https://apwu.org/news/alliance-began-brotherhood.

Berman, Edward. "Brotherhood of Sleeping Car Porters." Social Welfare History Project, February 27, 2018. https://socialwelfare.library.vcu.edu/eras/great-depression/brotherhood-of-sleeping-car-porters-win-over-pullman-company.

Chateauvert, Melinda. *Marching Together: Women of the Brotherhood of Sleeping Car Porters*. Urbana: University of Illinois Press, 1998.

Day, Meagan. "Labor: The First Black-Led Union Wouldn't Have Existed Without This Woman." 1199SEIU, June 19, 2018. http://www.1199seiu.org/media-center/daily-clips/labor-first-black-led-union-wouldnt-have-existed-without-woman.

Foner, Philip S., and Ronald L. Lewis, eds. *The Black Worker, Volume 6: The Era of Post-War Prosperity and the Great Depression, 1920-1936*. Temple University Press, 1981. https://doi.org/10.2307/j.ctvn5tvxv.

Harley, Sharon. *Sister Circle: Black Women and Work*. New Brunswick, NJ: Rutgers University Press, 2002.

Pitts, David. "Rosina Tucker—A Century of Commitment." United States Information Agency. February 8, 1996. https://usinfo.org/usia/usinfo.state.gov/usa/blackhis/rosina.htm.

Ah Quon McElrath

"Ah Quon McElrath." *AQ | Labor History Hawaii*. www.laborhistoryhawaii.org.

"CLEAR's Guide to Hawai'i Labor History." https://www.hawaii.edu/uhwo/clear/home/pdf/CLEAR_Hawaii_Labor_Hist_Pamphlet_2018.pdf.

"Hawaii activist Ah Quon McElrath dies at 92." Bizjournals.com. Accessed November 20, 2022. https://www.bizjournals.com/pacific/stories/2008/12/08/daily76.html.

Kelly, Kim. "Ah Quon McElrath and the Power of Multiracial Working-Class Solidarity." *The Nation*, January 28, 2022. http://www.thenation.com/article/activism/ah-quon-mcelrath-labor.

Mast, Robert H., and Anne B. Mast. *Autobiography of Protest in Hawaii*. University of Hawaii Press, 1997.

Parks, Shoshi. "The Not-so-Sweet Story of How Filipino Workers Tried to Take on Big Sugar in Hawaii." Medium, June 29, 2018. https://medium.com/timeline/filipino-workers-sugar-strike-fa58953e78e#:~:text=From%20the%20moment%20they%20began,infected%20patches%20on%20their%20necks.

"Pineapple Workers End Hawaii Strike," *New York Times*, July 17, 1947.

Reynolds, Mary Rebecca. "Red Lives: Grassroots Radicalism and Visionary Organizing in the American Century." EliScholar, 2021. https://elischolar.library.yale.edu/cgi/viewcontent.cgi?article=1105&context=gsas_dissertations.

Schwartz, Harvey. "Ah Quon McElrath: Service, Strength and Solidarity." ILWU, May 18, 2004. http://www.ilwu.org/ah-quon-mcelrath.

Takayama, Robynn. "Ah Quon McElrath, Hawaiian Strikes, Esp. 1946." Crossing East Archive, March 26, 2017. http://www.crossingeast.org/crossingeastarchive/2017/03/26/ah-quon-mcelrath-hawaiian-strikes-esp-1946.

Maria Moreno

Adios Amor: The Search for Maria Moreno (2018). Written and directed by Laurie Coyle. https://www.adiosamorfilm.com/.

Berkowitz, Bill. "Meet Maria Moreno: The First Farm Worker

Woman in America to Be Hired as a Union Organizer." Colorlines, February 28, 2018. https://colorlines.com/article/meet-maria-moreno-first-farm-worker-woman-america-be-hired-union-organizer.

Bloch, Sam. "You Already Know Cesar Chavez. What About Maria Moreno?" The Counter, September 23, 2019. https://thecounter.org/cesar-chavez-maria-moreno-ufw-awoc-farm-labor.

Feurer, Rosemary. "Talking for Justice! Maria Moreno/Migrant Women's Activism #LAWCHA19." LAWCHA, July 12, 2019. https://lawcha.org/2019/07/12/talking-for-justice-maria-moreno-migrant-womens-activism-lawcha19.

Kim, Inga. "The Rise of the UFW." UFW, January 20, 2023. https://ufw.org/the-rise-of-the-ufw.

Loomis, Erik. "Poverty in the Valley of Plenty." Lawyers, Guns & Money, January 5, 2016. https://www.lawyersgunsmoneyblog.com/2016/01/poverty-in-the-valley-of-plenty.

"Maria Moreno and Her Fight for America's Farmworkers." Latino Public Broadcasting. Accessed August 29, 2024. https://lpbp.org/maria-moreno-and-her-fight-for-americas-farmworkers.

Marks, Michael. "Documentary Uncovers the Lost History of Farmworker Activist Maria Moreno." Texas Standard, October 25, 2018. http://www.texasstandard.org/stories/documentary uncovers the-lost-history-of-farmworker-activist-maria-moreno.

Taylor, Ronald B. *Chavez and the Farm Workers*. Boston: Beacon Press, 1975.

Sue Ko Lee

"Labor Strike in Chinatown—Official Statements of Parties Involved, " *Chinese Digest*, April 1938, The Free Library. Accessed August 20, 2023. https://www.thefreelibrary.com/Labor+strike+in+Chinatown—official+statements+of+parties+involved%3A...-a0180315321.

Pesotta, Rose, "Subterranean Sweatshops in Chinatown." In *Bread Upon the Waters* (New York: Dodd, Mead, 1944).

Maytas, Jennie, "Letter to the editor," *Chinese Digest*, July 1937, p. 14.

"Sue Ko Lee." National Union of Healthcare Workers, March 22, 2022. https://nuhw.org/sue-ko-lee.

"Sue Ko Lee." U.S. National Park Service. Accessed August 20, 2023. http://www.nps.gov/people/sue-ko-lee.htm.

"Sue Ko Lee and the National Dollar Stores Strike of 1938." Library Exhibitions, City College of San Francisco, January 29, 2015. https://ccsfexhib.wordpress.com/2010/03/24/sue-ko-lee-and-the-national-dollar-stores-strike-of-1938.

"Sue Ko Lee Scrapbook on Chinese Ladies' Garment Workers' Union." Labor Archives Research Center, San Francisco State University. Accessed August 20, 2023. https://jpll.libraryhost.com/repositories/3/resources/522.

Ware, Susan. *Notable American Women: A Biographical Dictionary Completing the Twentieth Century*. Cambridge, MA: Harvard University Press, 2004.

Yung, Judy. *Unbound Feet: A Social History of Chinese Women in San Francisco*. Berkeley, CA: University of California Press, 1995.

Yung, Judy. *Unbound Voices: A Documentary History of Chinese Women in San Francisco*. Berkeley, CA: University of California Press, 1999.

Zheng, Heng Tang. "The Crisis in the Chinese Garment Industry and Its Future." Translated by John Qiu. *Chung Sai Yat Po*, April 10 and 11, 1935. https:// https://documents.alexanderstreet.com/d/1000678587.

Maida Springer Kemp

Kelly, Kim. "Maida Springer Kemp Championed Workers' Rights on a Global Scale." *The Nation*, February 6, 2022. https://www.thenation.com/article/activism/maida-springer-kemp-labor.

Prescod, Paul. "Maida Springer Insisted Unions Were Essential for Improving Black People's Lives." *Jacobin*. July 5, 2021. https://jacobin.com/2021/07/maida-springer-ilgwu-afl-cio-international-trade-unionism-africa-yevette-richards-us-labor.

Quinnell, Kenneth. "Women's History Month Profiles: Maida Springer Kemp." AFL-CIO, March 25, 2019. https://aflcio.org/2019/3/25/womens-history-month-profiles-maida-springer-kemp.

Richards, Yevette. *Maida Springer: Pan Africanist and International Labor Leader*. Pittsburgh: University of Pittsburgh Press, 2000.

Springer Kemp, Maida. Oral History Interview. #6036/024. Kheel Center for Labor-Management Documentation and Archives, Cornell University Library. https://rmc.library.cornell.edu/EAD/htmldocs/KCL06036-024.html.

Emma Tenayuca

Chacón, Justin Akers. *Radicals in the Barrio: Magonistas, Socialists, Wobblies, and Communists in the Mexican-American Working Class*. Chicago: Haymarket Books, 2018.

"Emma Tenayuca." National Park Service. Accessed June 20, 2022. http://www.nps.gov/people/emma-tenayuca.htm.

"Emma Tenayuca Becomes a Labor Organizer in San Antonio." Digital History. Accessed June 20, 2022. https://www.digitalhistory.uh.edu/disp_textbook.cfm?smtid=3&psid=3701.

"Emma Tenayuca: Hispanic, Mexican-Comanche, Civil Rights Activist, Labor Organizer, Educator, Communist, Pecan Strike." AmericansAll. Accessed June 20, 2022. https://americansall.org/legacy-story-individual/emma-tenayuca-0.

Kelly, Kim. "The Militant Passion of Emma Tenayuca." *The Nation*, February 1, 2022. http://www.thenation.com/article/activism/emma-tenayuca-labor.

Kelly, Kim. "Occupational Disease and Women: From the Radium Girls to Garment Workers." *Teen Vogue*, March 28, 2023.

http://www.teenvogue.com/story/occupational-disease-women.

Romo, Ricardo Dr. "Emma Tenayuca: A Warrior for Working Women," *La Prensa Texas*, March 12, 2021. https://laprensatexas.com/emma-tenayuca-a-warrior-for-working-women/.

Villegas, Jordan. "Emma Tenayuca: The Depression-Era Union Organizer Who Became 'La Pasionaria De Texas.'" *Latina*, May 19, 2021. https://latina.com/emma-tenayuca.

Dorothy Bolden

Beck, Elizabeth. "The National Domestic Workers Union and the War on Poverty." *The Journal of Sociology & Social Welfare* 28, no. 4 (December 2001). https://doi.org/10.15453/0191-5096.2772.

Boris, Eileen, and Premilla Nadasen. "Domestic Workers Organize!" *WorkingUSA* 11, no. 4 (November 2008): 413–37. https://doi.org/10.1111/j.1743-4580.2008.00217.x.

Bolden, Dorothy. "Dorothy Bolden Oral History." Interview by Chris Lutz. Special Collections and Archives, Georgia State University Library, Voices of Labor Oral History Collection, August 31, 1995. https://webapps.library.gsu.edu/ohms-viewer/viewer.php?cachefile=BoldenD_L1995-12_03.xml.

Chang, Grace. *Disposable Domestics: Immigrant Women Workers in the Global Economy*. Chicago: Haymarket Books, 2016.

Harrison, Christy Garrison. "They Led and a Community Followed: The Community Activism of Ella Mae Brayboy and Dorothy Bolden in Atlanta, Georgia, 1964–1994, 2007." MA thesis, Clark Atlanta University, 2007. https://radar.auctr.edu/islandora/object/cau.td:2007_harrison_christy_g.

Izsraael, Jacklyn. "How Dorothy Bolden Inspired the National Domestic Workers Bill of Rights." Medium, February 1, 2023. https://zora.medium.com/how-dorothy-bolden-inspired-the-national-domestic-workers-bill-of-rights-46ac8cdd0915.

"Life Story: Dorothy Bolden." Women & the American Story. Accessed February 1, 2023. https://wams.nyhistory.org/growth-and-turmoil/growing-tensions/dorothy-bolden/.

Slotnik, Daniel E. "Overlooked No More: Dorothy Bolden, Who Started a Movement for Domestic Workers." *New York Times*, February 20, 2019. https://www.nytimes.com/2019/02/20/obituaries/dorothy-bolden-overlooked.html.

Bayard Rustin

"Bayard Rustin." NBJC, March 17, 2017. https://beenhere.org/2017/03/17/bayard-rustin.

Bishop, Misun. "Lucille Campbell Green Randolph (1883–1963)." Blackpast, June 11, 2017. https://www.blackpast.org/african-american-history/randolph-lucille-campbell-green-1883-1963/.

Cochran, David. "The Lessons of A. Philip Randolph's Life for Racial Justice and Labor Activists Today." In These Times, March 1, 2016. https://inthesetimes.com/article/a-philip-randolph-march-on-washington.

D'Emilio, John. *Lost Prophet: The Life and Times of Bayard Rustin*. New York: Simon & Schuster, 2003.

Dixon, Mark E. "Bayard Rustin's Civil Rights Legacy Began with Grandmother Julia Rustin." Wayback Machine. Accessed August 20, 2023. https://web.archive.org/web/20181022232810/http://www.mainlinetoday.com/core/pagetools.php?pageid=10587&url=%2F-Main-Line-Today%2FOctober-2013%2FBayard-Rustins-Civil-Rights-Legacy-Began-with-Grandmother-Julia-Rustin%2F&mode=print.

Gude, Shawn. "The Tragedy of Bayard Rustin." Jacobin, May 23, 2018. https://jacobin.com/2018/05/the-tragedy-of-bayard-rustin.

Kirchick, James. "Odd Man Out." *The New Republic*, August 27, 2007. https://newrepublic.com/article/64446/odd-man-out.

"Memphis Sanitation Workers' Strike." The Martin Luther King, Jr. Research and Education Institute. Accessed August 20, 2023. https://kinginstitute.stanford.edu/memphis-sanitation-workers-strike.

"President Truman Ends Segregation in the Military." *HISTORY*, July 23, 2024. www.history.com/this-day-in-history/president-truman-ends-discrimination-in-military.

Randolph, A. Philip, and Bayard Rustin. "How the Civil-Rights Movement Aimed to End Poverty: A Freedom Budget for All Americans, Annotated." *The Atlantic*, December 12, 2022. http://www.theatlantic.com/magazine/archive/2018/02/a-freedom-budget-for-all-americans-annotated/557024.

"Rustin, Bayard." The Martin Luther King, Jr. Research and Education Institute. Accessed August 20, 2023. https//kinginstitute.stanford.edu/rustin-bayard.

Rustin, Bayard. *Time on Two Crosses: The Collected Writings of Bayard Rustin*. San Francisco: Cleis Press, 2014.

"Strike Supporters Bring in Outside Help." Memphis Public Libraries, July 6, 2018. https://www.memphislibrary.org/diversity/sanitation-strike-exhibit/sanitation-strike-exhibit-march-10-to-16-edition/strike-supporters-bring-in-outside-help.

Taylor, Cynthia. "The Men Behind the March: Randolph and Rustin Together Again." NYU Press, April 9, 2024. https://nyupress.org/blog/2013/08/27/the-men-behind-the-march-randolph-and-rustin-together-again.

Nagi Daifullah

Alamri, Neama. "Yemeni Farm Workers and the Politics of Arab Nationalism in the UFW." Boom California, February 8, 2020. https://boomcalifornia.org/2020/02/18/yemeni-farm-workers-and-the-politics-of-arab-nationalism-in-the-ufw/#_ftn29.

Alameri, Rua'a. "Brutal Killing That Made a Yemeni Immigrant

Hero of US Labor Movement." Al Arabiya, February 15, 2017. https://english.alarabiya.net/features/2017/02/15/Rediscovering-brave-but-tragic-legacy-of-Yemeni-immigrant-labor-leader-in-US-history.

Bisharat, Mary. "Yemeni Farmworkers in California." *MERIP Reports*, no. 34 (January 1975): 22–26. https://doi.org/10.2307/3011473.

Hebah Fisher, host, *Viva Brother Nagi,* podcast, season 3, episode 10, Kerning Cultures, February 15, 2023. https://kerningcultures.com/viva-brother-nagi/.

Hendricks, Tyche. "Legacy of Yemeni Immigrant Lives on Among Union Janitors / Farmworkers Organizer to Be Honored in S.F." SFGATE, August 16, 2002. https://www.sfgate.com/bayarea/article/Legacy-of-Yemeni-immigrant-lives-on-among-union-2782183.php.

Mansour, Omar. "Nagi Mohsin Daifullah and the Yemeni Farm Workers of California." *Arab America*, May 19, 2021. https://www.arabamerica.com/nagi-mohsin-daifullah-and-the-forgotten-yemeni-farmworkers-of-california.

Misra-Bhambri, Nikhil. "Yemenis in the San Joaquin Valley: The Embodiment of Pride, Duty and Loyalty." Arab American News, February 22, 2021. https://arabamericannews.com/2021/02/22/yemenis-in-the-san-joaquin-valley-the-embodiment-of-pride-duty-and-loyalty.

Riley, Annie. "Nagi Daifallah's Story Has Never Been More Important." The Yemeni American, August 13, 2017. https://yemeniamerican.com/en/nagi-daifallahs-story-has-never-been-more-important.

Judy Heumann

Cone, Kitty. "Short History of the 504 Sit-in," Disability Rights Education & Defense Fund, April 4, 2013. https://dredf.org/short-history-of-the-504-sit-in/.

"A Conversation with Judy Heumann on Independent Living." Disabled in Action of Metropolitan New York." Accessed August 23, 2023. https://www.disabledinaction.org/about-us/

beginnings/a-conversation-with-judy-heumann-on-independent-living/#independent.

"Disabled Tie Up Traffic Here to Protest Nixon Aid-Bill Vote." *New York Times*, November 3, 1972. https://www.nytimes.com/1972/11/03/archives/disabled-tie-up-traffic-here-to-protest-nixon-aidbill-vote.html.

"Examining 50 Years of the Rehabilitation Act of 1973—Section 504." U.S. Department of Labor Blog, July 26, 2023. https://blog.dol.gov/2023/07/26/examining-50-years-of-the-rehabilitation-act-of-1973-section-504.

Heumann, Judith, and Kristen Joiner. *Being Heumann: An Unrepentant Memoir of a Disability Rights Activist*. Boston: Beacon Press, 2020.

"Judy Heumann, Advocate for Rights of Disabled People." Accessed August 23, 2023. https://judithheumann.com/project/about.

Nielsen, Kim E. *A Disability History of the United States*. Boston: Beacon Press, 2012.

Shapiro, Joseph. "Activist Judy Heumann Led a Reimagining of What It Means to Be Disabled." NPR, March 5, 2023. https://www.npr.org/2023/03/04/1161169017/disability-activist-judy-heumann-dead-75.

Traub, Alex. "Judy Heumann, Who Led the Fight for Disability Rights, Dies at 75." *New York Times*, March 8, 2023. https://www.nytimes.com/2023/03/05/obituaries/judy-heumann-dead.html.

Silme Domingo and Gene Viernes

Chew, Ron. *Remembering Silme Domingo and Gene Viernes: The Legacy of Filipino American Labor Activism*. Alaskero Foundation, 2012.

Domingo, Cindy. "The Wards Cove Case: Separate and Unequal." *Positively Filipino*, October 28, 2013. https://www.positivelyfilipino.com/magazine/the-wards-cove-case-separate-and-unequal.

Gross, Ashley. "The Fight for Justice for Two Murdered Seattle

Men and How It Led to a Foreign Dictator." *KNKX Public Radio*, April 11, 2020. https://www.knkx.org/other-news/2020-04-11/the-fight-for-justice-for-two-murdered-seattle-men-and-how-it-led-to-a-foreign-dictator.

Kelly, Kim. "The Radical Vision of Silme Domingo and Gene Viernes." *The Nation*, January 19, 2022. https://www.thenation.com/article/society/domingo-viernes-union-reform.

Quinnell, Kenneth. *Asian Pacific American Heritage Month Profiles: Silme Domingo and Gene Viernes.* AFL-CIO, May 23, 2019. https://aflcio.org/2019/5/23/asian-pacific-american-heritage-month-profiles-silme-domingo-and-gene-viernes.

"Silme Domingo and Gene Viernes." Stanford Libraries, Rise up for Asian Americans and Pacific Islanders. Accessed August 25, 2023. https://exhibits.stanford.edu/riseup/feature/silme-domingo-gene-viernes.

Tilman, Robert O. "The Philippines in 1970: A Difficult Decade Begins." *Asian Survey* 11, no. 2 (February 1971): 139–48. https://doi.org/10.2307/2642713.

Joni Christian

Christian, Joni. "Transgender Lives: Your Stories: Joni Christian." *New York Times*, September 13, 2018. https://www.nytimes.com/interactive/2015/opinion/transgender-today/stories/joni-christian.

"Joni Christian. *LGBTQ Religious Archives Network*. Accessed June 23, 2023. https://lgbtqreligiousarchives.org/profiles/joni-christian.

McGinnis, Laura. "Working/Out: The Pride of the Labor Movement." U.S. Department of Labor Blog, June 3, 2021. https://web.archive.org/web/20240305020722/https://blog.dol.gov/2021/06/03/workingout-the-pride-of-the-labor-movement.

Quinnell. Kenneth. "Pride Month Profiles: Joni Christian." AFL-CIO, June 28, 2019. https://aflcio.org/2019/6/28/pride-month-profiles-joni-christian.

"Transgender Working People Have Needs. Is Your Union Meeting Them?" International Brotherhood of Teamsters. Accessed February 24, 2025. http://teamster.org/wp-content/uploads/2018/12/caucuslgbtqprideatwork.pdf.

Bhairavi Desai

Kelly, Kim. "What Drives Bhairavi Desai?" *Lux Magazine*, December 15, 2022. https://lux-magazine.com/article/bhairavi_desai_twa.

Khafagy, Amir. "New York Taxi Drivers Win Their Fight Against Medallion Debt." Documented, November 2021. https://documentedny.com/2021/11/05/new-york-taxi-drivers-win-their-fight-against-medallion-debt.

Massey, Daniel. "Bhairavi Desai." *Crain's New York Business*. Accessed August 24, 2023. https://www.crainsnewyork.com/awards/bhairavi-desai.

"Our Victories." New York Taxi Workers Alliance. Accessed August 24, 2023. https://www.nytwa.org/historic-victories.

Sharma, Kalpana. "September 11 and the Yellow Cabs." *The Hindu*, May 19, 2002. https://www.nriinternet.com/NRItaxi/USA/Union/Bhairavi%20Desai/0_co-founder.htm.

Wadler, Joyce. "PUBLIC LIVES; An Unlikely Organizer as Cabdrivers Unite." *New York Times*, December 8, 1999. https://www.nytimes.com/1999/12/08/nyregion/public-lives-an-unlikely-organizer-as-cabdrivers-unite.html.

Wishnia, Steve. "After Suicides and Hunger Strikes, Underwater Cabbies Win Loan Guarantees From City." *LaborPress*, November 4, 2021. https://www.laborpress.org/after-suicides-and-hunger-strikes-underwater-cabbies-win-loan-guarantees-from-city.

Jennifer Bates

Kim Kelly. Interviews with Jennifer Bates, 2021–2022 (in-person in Birmingham, AL, and via phone). Kim Kelly's archives.

"Jennifer Bates, BAmazon Spokesperson, Reinstated by Amazon in Stunning Win." RWDSU press release, June 15, 2023. https://www.rwdsu.org/news/jennifer-bates-bamazon-union-spokesperson-reinstated-by-amazon-in-stunning-win-for-workers.

"Jennifer Bates, 'Bamazon Worker-leader' Reinstated by Amazon Is a Win for Workers." UNI Global Union, June 20, 2023. https://uniglobalunion.org/news/jennifer-win.

Kelly, Kim. "An Unholy Union." Vox, March 22, 2021. https://www.vox.com/the-highlight/22320009/amazon-bessemer-union-rwdsu-alabama.

Kelly, Kim. "Endings and Beginnings in Bessemer." Strikewave, April 15, 2021. https://www.thestrikewave.com/original-content/endings-and-beginnings-in-bessemer?fbclid=IwY2xjawGsf3VleH-RuA2FlbQIxMAABHYPNlm2VsAtAVODd7ecWSuq-A8irL-rAz_YI1BAGwArewnjG6zdN3DrBlaA_aem_FFlHVZwJhaaKX9d-VsL-Beg.

PHOTOS

BEN FLETCHER, a dockworker, labor organizer, and political activist who opposed racism and capitalism, helped form a strong, interracial union on the Philadelphia waterfront, and later faced government repression.

FRANCES PERKINS, a lifelong advocate for worker safety who witnessed the Triangle Shirtwaist Factory Fire, later became the first female secretary of labor and was a primary architect behind the New Deal.

LUCY PARSONS, a labor organizer and political activist, was born into slavery in Virginia and later became one of the most famous anarchists in America. The Chicago police considered her "more dangerous than a thousand rioters."

MOTHER JONES, an Irish immigrant, became a labor organizer for the United Mine Workers and was a self-described "hellraiser" who struck fear into the hearts of crooked politicians and bad bosses alike.

MOTHER JONES AND HER "ARMY" of mill children marched from Philadelphia to President Theodore Roosevelt's Long Island summer home in 1903 to protest child labor.

EUGENE V. DEBS, a labor organizer and political activist, advocated for socialism. When the government arrested him for speaking out against World War I, he ran for president from his prison cell.

BAYARD RUSTIN, a gay civil rights activist, organized the 1963 March on Washington for Jobs and Freedom and later became involved in international political movements.

TWO WOMEN GARMENT WORKERS on strike for higher wages and better working conditions in the early 1900s.

ABOUT THE AUTHOR

Kim Kelly is a labor reporter for *In These Times* magazine and has been a regular labor columnist for *Teen Vogue* since 2018. Her writing on labor, class, politics, disability, and culture has appeared in *The Nation*, the *Washington Post*, the *New York Times*, *The Baffler*, *The New Republic*, *Rolling Stone*, *Esquire*, and many others. Kelly has also worked as a video correspondent for More Perfect Union, the Real News Network, and Means TV. Previously she was the heavy metal editor at *Noisey*, *VICE*'s former music vertical, and helped to organize the *VICE* Union. A third-generation union member, she served three terms as an elected councilperson for the Writers Guild of America, East Council. Her first book, *Fight Like Hell: The Untold History of American Labor*, was published in 2022. She was born in the heart of the South Jersey Pine Barrens and currently lives in Philadelphia with a hardworkin' man, a couple of taxidermied bears, and way too many books.